Be a Woman of Faith

By
Deborah S. Moore

Kingdom
Ministry Publications
877-286-6372
www.kingdomgroup.net

BE A WOMAN OF FAITH
ISBN 978-0-9823390-0-8

Deborah S Moore

P.O. BOX 53
OWOSSO, MI 48867
WWW.GNI.GLOBAL

Published by:

Kingdom
Ministry Publications
877-286-6372
www.kingdomgroup.net

❧ CONTENTS ❧

ᘒ FOREWORD ᘏ
by Larry Huggins, D.D.

The New Testament has examples of women of faith: Elizabeth, Eunice, Joanna, Lois, Mary, Priscilla, Susanna — to name a few. Debbie Moore is a modern-day woman of faith. During the decades that I have been a friend and colleague of the Moore's, I have marveled at Debbie's resolute faith – a faith that has buoyed her family and friends during the tempests of life. There's a lot to be learned from a woman of faith such as Debbie Moore.

I saw what she's made of as she and her husband, Jan, took a hard field and pioneered Good News Church. I saw what she's made of as she raised seven Godly children, and passed to them her legacy of faith. I saw what she's made of when she refused to lose her house. I saw what she's made of as she courageously held fast to her comatose son, Joseph, the victim of a freakish house-explosion that took the lives of six children. God raised him up! I saw what she's made of as she and her husband, Jan, stood against the heartless, Goliath-sized utility company that denied responsibility for the explosion that rocked a community, and sent Debbie and her family to their knees. Justice prevailed!

This is not theoretical faith; it's real faith, tested in the crucible of life — the kind of faith that will get a woman, a wife, a mother through the hard places.

I goaded Debbie a little about writing a book: she was a little reluctant to write it. However, you will see, you can learn a lot from a woman of faith such as Debbie Moore.

This book is dedicated to my mother Lois who first taught me the joy and honor of being a woman and showed me, by her example, a life lived hungering and thirsting after God.

❧ INTRODUCTION ❧

Yes, be a woman of faith. Put your all on the line for the One who gave His all for you. Dare to believe the dream in your heart, the hope that you cling to. Let faith arise in your heart to be all that He has designed you to be. Allow Him to move in your life supernaturally, completely, perhaps for the first time. Step out in faith, believing Him at His Word. Don't depend on anything else, but that He loves you and His Word is true. Don't allow doubt to overtake you this time. Don't fall back on old habits or other sources. Believe that God will do it, and let Him be your sole source. Step out into what seems like thin air, and feel the Solid Rock beneath your feet!

Allow the Holy Spirit to be your guide, not guilt or pressure or the desire to please people. Listen as He speaks to you in that gentle, unmistakable voice or that solid, reassuring tone as He leads you in this great adventure of life. Don't be just what you want to be – be what He wants you to be. And you will find yourself in that life abundant that you didn't know existed. You've heard of it, you've seen glimpses of it, now step into it!

❧ CHAPTER 1 ❧
FAITH PLEASES GOD

"But without faith it is impossible to please him: for he that cometh to God must believe that he is, and that he is a rewarder of them that diligently seek Him."

Hebrews 11:6

All my life I have wanted to please God. I went to church seeking a way to make myself worthy of His attention or answers to my prayers. I taught Sunday School and sang in the choir and led youth group and went to camp. I prayed and read my Bible and talked about God with anyone who had a listening ear. Then one day I learned that God is pleased by simply believing – believing that He is God! Simple, childlike faith pleases God. Faith that trusts the goodness of our Heavenly Father pleases God. We believe in the ability of our Father who showed the unfathomable riches of His love when He gave His only begotten Son to die for us, that pleases God.

In fact, without faith it is impossible to please God. All our efforts at working for Him are fruitless without that simple faith. We must have faith in order to be pleasing to God. Our walk with God must be a walk of faith, the God kind of faith. I want to encourage you to begin your walk of faith, continue in your walk of faith and grow in your walk of faith. Regardless of your condition or position or persuasion, if you believe God and want to live a life pleasing to Him, you must operate according to the Word He has given us. Through His Word He reveals to us who He is and who we are in Him. As a woman, you are to take your place in His Kingdom, bearing fruit that is pleasing to Him and fulfilling the destiny He has in mind for you. Many times we make excuses – blaming the time in our life, circumstances around us, our husband's lack of faith or our lack of a husband! God expects us to walk in faith — period. Regardless of your marital status or the condition of your spouse's walk with God, you must still walk by faith.

Hebrews 11:1 gives us the definition of faith. "Now faith is the substance of things hoped for, the evidence of things not seen." Consider that for a moment. Faith is substance. It is real. Faith is evidence of things that have not come to pass. It is the substance of things we are hoping for, it is the evidence of things in the future. Just as God made Adam out of the dust of the earth, faith is the substance from which your hopes are brought into being. Faith brings those hopes into reality. But this faith goes beyond the power of positive thinking. It is more than the little train who said, "I think I can. I think I can. I think I can." Faith is the spiritual substance that connects us with the supernatural power of God. God takes our faith and uses it to make our dreams come true. Faith moves us from the realm of the natural into the supernatural.

It opens a new dimension to us. It allows us to see into the future, to look beyond what we see in front of us to what is possible ahead. Faith looks beyond lack to see provision. Faith looks beyond sickness and disease to see healing. Faith looks beyond the problem to the power of God. Faith makes the connection with that power and there's a miracle!

The Bible says that through faith we understand that the worlds were framed by the Word of God (Hebrews 11:3). We will look at this more closely in a later chapter, but according to the Word, this world was brought into being by the voice of God commanding light, water, dry land, to appear. In the first chapter of Genesis it is recorded that He said, "Let there be..." and there was! "Let there be light"– and there was light. "Let there be Heaven"– and there were the heavens above us. "Let the dry land appear"– and there were the continents we travel. Out of a formless void, out of emptiness, all that we see around us was brought into being by the power of God. This same power is at work in your life, bringing into reality those things which may seem to be nothing but dreams. By faith we understand that this is how God operates. He can bring something out of nothing.

By faith Abraham believed God and was counted righteous (Romans 4:3). What did Abraham believe? He believed in God Who had spoken to him, and that God's promise of a son was true, even though Abraham was a 75-year-old man when God first told him that a son would be born to him and Sarah (Genesis 15:5). The Bible describes Abraham's faith in Romans 4:19-21. First, he was not weak in faith. He had grown in his relationship with God, knowing that God was able to fulfill His promise. In the strength of his faith, he did not consider his own body, now dead – that is unable to father a child, neither yet the deadness of Sarah's womb but grew strong in faith giving glory to God. The birth of a child to this elderly couple was a physical impossibility. Nevertheless, Abraham chose to believe God rather than the circumstances that were completely contrary to this promise. Verse 20 says that Abraham did not waver in his faith. He didn't believe one minute and doubt the next, but rather he grew strong in faith as he continued to give glory to God. Abraham's faith connected with the power of God and he had a son, Isaac.

This faith is a gift from God given to us at salvation. "For by grace you have been saved through faith, and that not of yourselves, it is the gift of God, not of works, lest anyone should boast." (Ephesians 2:8-9) This gift is given us to begin our relationship with God, and God requires us to use this gift for the rest of our lives. As we read earlier, this is the faith that pleases God. Isn't it wonderful that God gives it to us as a gift! He places it within our hearts so that we can respond to Him when He knocks on the door and asks us to let Him in (Revelation 3:20). So this faith is the gift that keeps on giving – as we grow and increase in our knowledge of God. We began our journey as Christians with this faith, so we continue to grow in Him and in faith; as the Bible says, "...your faith groweth exceedingly," (II Thessalonians 1:3). We are to grow and develop in faith, not remaining babies but growing in grace and in the knowledge of God.

Paul's letter to the Romans describes that first step as Christians. "But what does it say? 'The word is near you, in your mouth and in your heart,' (that is, the word of faith which we preach): that if you confess with your mouth the Lord Jesus and believe in your heart that God has raised Him from the dead, you will be saved." (Romans 10:8-9) You confess with your mouth that Jesus is Lord and believe in your heart that God raised Him from the dead, you will be saved. Faith works the same way throughout your walk with Christ. You believe in your heart that "by His stripes you are healed" and you confess with your mouth that you are healed. You believe in your heart, "the Lord is my Shepherd, I shall not want," and you confess with your mouth that you will not lack because God will take care of you. It is really very simple. You believe in your heart and confess with your mouth. How do you know what to believe? You read the Bible!

The first thing you must believe, according to Hebrews 11:6, is that God exists and that He is a rewarder of those who diligently seek Him. That is the first step. For years philosophers have been saying that God is dead. Others try to persuade us that God is simply a good force in the universe, or that He is whoever you want Him to be. If you want to enjoy a relationship of intimate communion and life-giving power, you must believe that God is alive, that there is a God. And not only that He is alive, that He exists, that He is – but that He is a rewarder of those who diligently seek Him. That brings us to another mindset we must change. How many people think of God as a celestial judge, waiting to punish us for what we have done? How many people use His Name to curse others or things? But God's Word says He is a rewarder of those who diligently seek Him. He is a rewarder! He has good things for His children. If you were brought up not knowing God, or thinking only of Him as the judge who would punish your wrongdoings, you must understand that He is a rewarder of those who diligently seek Him. His plans for you are for good and not for evil (Jeremiah 29:11). Jesus said He came to give us life and that more abundantly! (John 10:10) He has good things ahead for you! James 1:17 says, "Every good gift and every perfect gift is from above, and cometh down from the Father of lights, with whom is no variableness, neither shadow of turning." God is a good God. He gives us good things. So faith lifts us up into a new way of looking at life. We can see it as a path full of promise from God. We don't have to fear the future, we face the future with confidence, knowing that we are in God's hands and that He has good things ahead.

Looking at this verse again, we see that God is a rewarder of those who diligently seek Him. This walk of faith is a daily walk, not one to pick up when you need God and then cast aside when everything is going all right. You must diligently, day in and day out, seek Him. This is how you learn to know God and to grow in faith in Him. Through good times and bad, when life is easy or the days are hard, as you seek God you will find strength to help in time of need. He loves you completely and knows exactly what you need for everyday! (Matthew 6:32) No matter what the day may bring, God already knows about it and has a plan to help you through it. We find amazing strength throughout the routines of life, the storms of life, the surprises of life and the delights of life if we diligently seek God. Then as you spend time with Him each day, you become more intimately acquainted with Him and learn how to respond to Him in faith – which pleases Him!

There are many accounts in the gospels giving record of miracles that happened through Jesus' ministry. Many times as people came to Him in need of a healing miracle, Jesus replied, "According to your faith be it unto you." Or "Your faith has made you whole." These individuals came to Jesus with the simple belief that He could do the impossible. He could meet the great need in their lives. He could change their lives. That simple faith met Jesus – God in the flesh – and their miracle occurred. Blind eyes opened, deaf ears heard, lame legs walked, the dead were raised to life – all as a result of simple faith, believing that Jesus could do a miracle. Now, faith is the vital ingredient to receiving the miracle you need. God wants you to believe Him. Believe that He can and will do as He has promised. Your miracle is on its way!

Finally, faith is the commodity that Jesus will be looking for when He returns. It is one thing that will endure. "Now abideth faith, hope and love..." (I Corinthians 13:13). Faith abides, it stays, it remains solid and unshakeable to keep us through every difficulty, every hard place, every test and trial. In the end, Jesus will be looking for faith when He returns. (Luke 18:8) In that day, will He find our hearts full of faith, trusting and believing until the end? Yes! He will find faith in me!

ଓ CHAPTER 2 ଓ
WOMAN OF THE WORD

"So then faith cometh by hearing, and hearing by the Word of God."

Romans 10:17

To be a woman of faith, you must be a woman of the Word. The Bible is the revelation of God to man. He shows us who He is in the pages of this wonderful Book. To know God, you must know His Word. The Bible declares that He has magnified His Word above His Name (Psalm 138:2). Jesus said that heaven and earth would pass away, but not one dot of an "i" or crossing of a "t" would pass away. He said He did not come to do away with the Word, but to fulfill it. (Matthew 5:17-18) The Word is the foundation to our relationship with God. Through the Word, we come into this relationship of salvation, and learn what it is to walk as a child of God. Through the Word we learn that we can call God "Father". Through the Word we learn how to pray, we learn how to live, and we learn how to relate to God. There is no getting around it, you must be a student of the Word if you really want to know God and walk with Him on this earth.

We must understand that the Bible is the Word of God. It is not just another book, it is not just a history book or a compilation of writings, it is the Word of God to us today. It is an eternal book. The Bible says that the Word is forever settled in heaven (Psalm 119:89). Jesus said that heaven and earth would pass away but His Word would never pass away (Matthew 5:17). This book is more than just a book, it is the Word of God, as Hebrews 4:12 says, "alive and powerful, sharper than any two-edged sword, able to divide asunder between soul and spirit and joints and marrow, and is a discerner of the thoughts and intents of the heart." The Word is alive! It is not just the words on the page that you read, it is alive and powerful, able to see and discern the very thoughts of your heart. When you read this Word, you are reading a book that can change your life, change your very nature as you allow it to do its work. As we read the Word, we must receive it as God speaking to us. II Timothy 3:16-17 says that "all scripture is given by inspiration of God and is profitable for doctrine, for reproof, for correction, for instruction in righteousness that the man of God may be perfect, thoroughly furnished unto all good works." All scripture is God-breathed, authored by the Creator of the universe as He worked through men to show us who He is and how He has moved through the ages to demonstrate His great love for us. When we come to the Word, we must allow God to speak to us through these pages, receiving His Truth in our spirit. The Word is our instruction. We don't come to the Bible to analyze and dissect it to see whether it fits our theology, we come with open hearts to hear what the Lord will say to us today. We receive it as God sitting in the room, speaking to us the things we need to hear.

Romans 15:4 says, "For whatsoever things were written aforetime were written for our learning, that we through patience and comfort of the scriptures might have hope." We are to learn the Word of God. How wonderful that through the study of the Word we find patience and comfort in the scriptures! Walking by faith is not easy, but when you go to the Word you receive strength in the battles you may be facing. We know that in the end we win, but in the meantime we may be going through some things. In the middle of the difficulty, we can turn to the scriptures where we will find patience to wait upon God and comfort to shield our hearts from hurt and disappointment. And through these scriptures we have hope! Things will get better! "Weeping may endure for a night, but joy cometh in the morning!" (Psalm 30:5) We have hope through these same scriptures; hope that the future will be brighter and the dreams in our hearts will come to pass. We have hope! Even beyond this life, beyond the finality of death, we have the hope of eternal life in the presence of God in Heaven. We walk by faith; we have this hope within us. This hope comes from the Word of God. It is not just a good feeling; it is a truth from the Word that endures. It stands the test of time. The Bible says hope does not disappoint us. (Romans 5:5) God will not let you down. He will never fail you.

Paul's instructions to Timothy, his co-worker, are to "study to show yourself approved unto God, a workman that needeth not to be ashamed, rightly dividing the Word of truth." (II Timothy 2:15) Why do we need to spend time in the

Word? We spend time in the Word so that we can be good students, approved by God. As we study the Word the Lord brings revelation to us which causes us to walk in a way that is pleasing to Him. We will not be ashamed or embarrassed, but we will understand what God is saying to us. It takes time in the Word to be a good student. And we have the best Teacher, the Holy Spirit, who takes the Word and brings revelation and understanding to us. God does not play a guessing game with us. If we read and study His Word, He will show us the truth of who He is and who we are in Him. He will reveal to us His plan for our lives as we seek Him and spend time in His Word. David said that the Word is a lamp to my feet and a light to my path. (Psalm 119:105) We can see the steps ahead of us if we will spend time with God and spend time in His Word.

Romans 10:17 instructs us that faith comes by hearing and hearing by the Word of God. In order to be a woman of faith and to grow in faith you must keep yourself in the Word of God. Notice the Scripture says faith comes by hearing – that is continuing to hear the Word of God. Sometimes when we hear a familiar message, or a scripture, there is the temptation to think, "That's nothing new. I've heard that before." But this passage says that faith comes by hearing – and hearing and hearing and hearing! God continues to bring revelation to us as we open our hearts to His Word. Walking in faith is challenging! You are walking in opposition to this world and its system. You use your faith in the rigors of daily life, and you must keep yourself in the Word to keep your faith strong. When you feel taxed, sapped of strength, you have only to go to the Word of God to be renewed. You don't need to pray and ask God for more faith; you only need to go to the Word, because faith comes by hearing the Word of God.

You must build your faith upon the foundation of the Word of God, and nothing else. You cannot build on your own ideas or what you have been taught in the past. You cannot build upon the foundation of what someone has told you. You must go to the Word of God, the Bible, to find the truth. You must read it for yourself. Then regardless of life's storms, your house will not fall. In Matthew 7:24-27, Jesus gives us a clear picture of two men, one built his house upon a rock. The Bible says the storm came, the rain descended, the floods came, the winds blew and beat on the house – and the house did not fall. In contrast, another man built his house on the sand. Jesus calls this man foolish, for the same storm came upon his house and it fell because it was built upon the sand. What was the difference between the two – the foundation upon which they built. Jesus describes the rock foundation as hearing and obeying the Word. The sand foundation is hearing the Word but doing nothing to put it into practice. The Word of God must be the rock upon which you build your life. Notice that both men heard the Word, but the wise one acted on what he heard. His home withstood the storm because he did according to the instruction and direction from the Word. This is vital to walking by faith. You must believe God and believe His Word and then act upon that belief.

To be a woman of faith requires that you begin to walk according to the Word of God, and not according to the world around you. The book of James says that we must be doers of the Word and not hearers only. (James 1:22) He goes on to say that when we only hear the Word and don't respond by obeying it, we deceive ourselves. We deceive ourselves! We open the door to wrong thoughts and ideas and presumptions about God when we only hear the Word and don't act on it. The Bible is not just another book about God – it is God's own Word to us! We cannot approach it with a "take it or leave it" attitude. We must receive it as God's Word to us that gives us instruction and direction for the way we live today. Walking according to the Word of God means that as you read every precious Word, you allow it to mold your thinking and attitude and actions. You learn to walk by what the Bible says, not the way you have walked in the past, or the way everyone else walks. We read the Bible, and then do what it says!

Jesus said that we are in the world, but not of the world. (John 17:16) In other words, we still live on this wonderful earth God has given us, but we do not belong to this world. We are citizens of the Kingdom of Heaven. We have been adopted into the family of God by virtue of the blood of Jesus. We can walk in this world as children of God, kings and priests unto God. We are not limited by our own ability; we have the power of God available to us. And we learn about Him by studying His Word. We learn about who we are in Him by studying His Word. Let me reiterate, you can't build the foundation of your life upon what someone told you that the Bible says. You must read it for yourself and hear it for yourself. Then you will be able to know and understand the things that God has for you.

As you read and study the Word, you will know God as you have never known Him before. He brings you revelation of the meaning of His Word, and He reveals Himself to you in fresh and new ways. It is fulfilling and wonderful, to walk this walk of faith with God. No matter how long you may have known Him, there is more to know! The love relationship we share grows deeper and more intimate with each passing day as we walk in this life of faith.

Perhaps this is a way of life you have never known before. Many Christians live their lives thinking that God is up in heaven just watching and waiting for us to join Him, hoping that somehow we will make it through this life on earth. Nothing could be further from the truth! The Bible declares that through the power of God, we are given all things pertaining to life and godliness. (II Peter 1:3) And that means all things that pertain to this life and our spiritual development. God is aware of the requirements to live this life. Jesus said that we should have such trust in our Father's care for us that we don't even have to think about how we are to obtain the basic necessities of life. "Therefore do not worry, saying, 'What shall we eat?' or 'What shall we drink?' or 'What shall we wear?' For after all these things the Gentiles seek. For your heavenly Father knows that you need all these things. But seek first the kingdom of God and His righteousness, and all these things shall be added to you." (Matthew 6:31-33) By faith we trust the Word of God that reveals to us the care of our heavenly Father who "knows that you need all these things." By His power we are given all things that pertain to life and godliness. We are instructed to seek first the kingdom of God and trust that all these things will be added to us. This is walking in faith! Jesus Himself declared that He came to give us life, and to give it to us abundantly. (John 10:10) This abundant life comes when we walk in faith with God, looking for miracles everyday. We live expecting God's hand to move in our lives as we look beyond the natural realm into the supernatural, considering the power and ability of God to change the things before us.

We can walk in this world as children of God, kings and priests unto God. We are not limited as the rest of the world. We have the resources of heaven, the power and the authority of the Name of Jesus, and the power of the Blood of Jesus. We can call upon God for help. In fact, He invites us into His throne room to "find grace to help in time of need!" (Hebrews 4:16) Glory to God! We must rise up as women of God, women of faith, and believe God for miracles all around us!

But you will not know the authority that you have as a believer, the power that is available to you, the power that God has given you; if you do not read the Word. We have the truth of the Word to take us through any situation. Jesus said, "If you continue in My Word, then are ye My disciples indeed, and you shall know the truth and the truth shall set you free." (John 8:32) We are familiar with parts of that verse, namely, "the truth shall set you free." But Jesus has set some qualifications before we come into that freedom. First we must continue in His Word, continue. That means day in and day out stay in the Word of God. Don't just begin in an emotional moment and then quit. No! Continue in the Word of God. If you continue in the Word – then you are His disciples. You aren't a disciple just because you call yourself one. You are a disciple when you continue in His Word. Then you will know the truth. What is truth? Jesus said, "I am the Way, the Truth and the Life. No man comes to the Father but by Me." (John 14:6) Jesus is the Truth. You will know the truth. You will know God and His power, and that truth will set you free.

Now as I have taught on the importance of studying the Word, I have had people approach me saying they just don't understand the Bible. It's hard for them to sit and read the Bible. Let me say that there are countless modern versions of the Bible available to you. Find one that you can understand.

I love the King James Version, but there are other versions that are in today's language and not Elizabethan English! They are accurate and easy to read. But the most important thing to remember about reading the Bible is to be in an attitude of prayer and communication with God as you are reading. God will speak to you through the Word that you read. Daily you will be built up so that you are growing stronger and stronger in Him. If you don't understand a portion, ask God to help you! He is right there with you as you are reading, and He will speak to your heart to help you understand His wonderful Word. As Jesus was teaching His disciples, preparing them for His departure from this life, He told them about the Holy Spirit who would be with them. Jesus said, "He will teach you all things and lead you into all truth." (John 16:13) When you become a child of God, the Holy Spirit is on the inside of you. He will teach you and lead you into the truth of God's Word. Don't use that old excuse, "the Bible is so hard to understand." God has given us His Word and His Spirit to help us to know Him and to live successfully in this life. Also, you must remember that the devil doesn't want you to read the Word. He will try to get you thinking about other things, distracting you from focusing on the Word. He will try to confuse you with questions to try to discourage you from reading the Word. So you must resist the devil and continue to read the Word. God will bring understanding to your heart as you read.

Rev. Terry Mize, a dear friend and wonderful man of God, an apostle to the nations of the world, says, "I know that God is good and I know His Word is Truth." It is vitally important that we know that the Word of God is the truth. As Rev. Mize says, it may be true that the devil is picking on you, you may have problems you are facing; but the truth is that in the end – we win! The truth is, according to the Word of God, "nay, in all these things we are more than conquerors through Him who loved us." (Romans 8:37) This is the diligence we must apply to our daily lives while walking in faith. We look at our problem and then we look at the Word and find the answer. Then instead of continuing to focus on our problem, we focus on the word that God has given us. For example, if you have a financial need, (and who doesn't!), you choose to focus on God's Word which promises, "My God shall supply all your need according to His riches in glory by Christ Jesus." (Philippians 4:19) Now it is true that you have bills. It is true that you have a financial need, but the Truth is, "My God shall supply all your need according to His riches in glory by Christ Jesus." When you walk by faith, you choose to focus on the promises of God rather than the problem. You believe God and trust His Word to you.

Look at Luke 7:1-10 and the account of a Roman centurion who heard of Jesus. This centurion had a servant who was grievously ill. He knew that Jesus could heal his servant, but he was concerned that Jesus should not be seen in his home. This centurion knew authority. He was a soldier. He knew how to give orders and how to follow orders. He believed Jesus' words had authority to command. He said to Jesus, "Say the word and my servant shall be healed." When Jesus heard this, He said this kind of faith was unsurpassed in Israel; this kind of faith that believes in the authority of the Word of God. Of course, the centurion received the miracle he needed. His servant was healed the moment Jesus spoke the word. This is faith! In fact, Jesus marveled at this kind of faith — faith in the heart of a Roman who believed the Word of God.

When you have any need or problem in your life, you have only to go to the Word of God to find the answer. It is a choice you make continually. You choose to cling to the promises of God, to stand upon the Rock of His Word, rather than give in to the torment of worry and fear. All our "what if's" boil down to fear over the future. And the Bible says, "There is no fear in love; but perfect love casteth out fear: because fear hath torment. He that feareth is not made perfect in love." (I John 4:18) When we make the faith decision to depend on the power of God and His Word, His perfect love casts out our fear. How can we fear the future when God has already shown His perfect love for us through the priceless gift of His Son? All our "what if's" have already been answered in the Word, and the love of God as shown in Jesus, His Son.

"What if I lose my job?" "My God shall supply all your need according to His riches in glory by Christ Jesus." (Philippians 4:19)

"What if I get sick with cancer, or some other disease?" "He Himself took our infirmities and carried our diseases, by whose stripes you were healed." (Isaiah 53:5)

"I can't handle my children." "All your children shall be taught of the Lord and great shall be your peace." (Isaiah 54:13)

"What if my husband leaves me?" "God will never leave you or forsake you." (Hebrews 13:5)

We refuse to fear in the face of any situation, knowing that the answer is found in the Word of God. We know that the Word of God is Truth, regardless of the difficulty.

As a woman of faith, this is the way I live my life, "looking not at the things which are seen, but at the things which are unseen." (II Corinthians 4:18) I don't allow the limitations of the natural world to dictate to me what God can or can't do in my life or the lives of those around me. I use my faith to reach out to God, make a faith-connection, and watch His hand perform miracles! This is the kind of faith I am talking about in this book. As I John states, "This is the victory that overcomes the world, even our faith."! (I John 5:4)

☙ CHAPTER 3 ❧
You Are a Woman of Faith

"Therefore if any man be in Christ, he is a new creature: old things are passed away; behold, all things are become new."

II Corinthians 5:17

If we are in Christ, we are new creatures. The Bible says that old things have passed away, all things have become new. (II Corinthians 5:17) No matter what has happened in your past, God has made you new in Him. You are a brand new being. You can take the hand of God and make a new path for yourself as you follow Him. This is a great part of the faith walk, realizing that the old is gone and the fresh and new has come. We must let go of yesterday and walk today with God. Oral Roberts says, "God is in the now!" He is the same yesterday, today and forever!

You must begin to look at yourself the way the Word describes you, rather than the way you have always seen yourself. When you are in Christ, you are a new creature, a new kind of being altogether. Jesus said that you are born again. (John 3:3) Each day is a brand new day for you when you are in Christ Jesus. There is a new world open to you. You must see yourself as a beautiful woman of God, tenderly loved and dearly prized by the Creator of the Universe. He loves you so much that He gave His only begotten Son to make the way for you to be accepted back into His family. Remember, Adam and Eve were expelled from the Garden of Eden because of their sin. They were separated from God. All of creation was subject to death. But through the sacrifice of Jesus on the cross, the way has been made for us to come back to the Father. He is waiting with open arms to welcome you home! Jesus' blood is more than powerful enough to cleanse you from every sin. Your past is over and done. The transaction is complete. Paul describes us as being "dead" to the things of the past, our sin and limitations, and now "alive" unto God. (Romans 6:11) You must see yourself as a new person altogether. The world is a cruel one. Many women suffer many kinds of abuses. And there is always that little voice continually saying you can't, you're not good enough, etc. When you begin this life in Christ, you are free from the past completely. You are free to live a new life unto God – a life pleasing to Him. As Jesus stood before the woman caught in adultery, He asked her, "Where are your accusers?" When she looked around, she could see none. He replied, "Neither do I condemn you. Go and sin no more." (John 8:3-11) His forgiveness was complete. She had an opportunity to begin her life anew. She had been promiscuous, a woman living in sin. The whole town knew who she was and the kind of life she led. But at that wonderful moment, Jesus gave her an opportunity to begin again, without guilt or condemnation, and with the urging that she use this opportunity to change her life. When you experience God's forgiveness, you are free to follow Him. The chains of the past are broken by His power. He urges you and expects you to use this new freedom as an opportunity to change your life and to live in a way which brings glory to His Name.

The Bible says that Jesus became sin for us, Jesus Who knew no sin, the perfect One, became sin for us. Why? So that we might be made the righteousness of God in Him. "For He hath made Him to be sin for us, Who knew no sin; that we might be made the righteousness of God in Him." (II Corinthians 5:21) Jesus, the spotless Lamb of God, the perfect One, the One who had never sinned, never made a mistake, never failed; literally became sin for you and me. The sin of the world was placed upon Him during that holy sacrifice upon the cross. In those moments He became sin so that you and I might become the righteousness of God – the righteousness of God! This righteousness is the character or quality of being right or just. God allows us to come into right relationship with Him, not because of what we have done but because of the sacrificial gift that God gave us in His Son. Isaiah says that all our righteousness is as filthy rags. (Isaiah 64:6) All our efforts at being right, compared to God's righteousness, look like dirty rags. So God in His wonderful mercy gave His only begotten Son as a sacrifice for you and me. The perfect One was offered for you and me, and in return we are made the righteousness of God! The next time the enemy tells you you're not good enough, that God won't hear or answer your prayer because you just don't measure up – quote this verse. You are made the very righteousness of God! He has qualified you to be a partaker of the inheritance of the saints in light! (Colossians 1:12) We could not do it. We could not live in a way that would prove to be worthy of God's acceptance. So God made the way Himself, through the blood of His own Son. It is by faith in Him, receiving Him as your Savior that you experience this transforming power. His blood washes you completely clean. He declares that you are now righteous, not with any righteousness that you have earned, but with His righteousness; the righteousness of God.

I want you to understand the importance of this truth. One tactic of the enemy is to make you feel that you can never be good enough to have your prayers answered, that you must somehow qualify for a miracle. How many times do we read of ordinary people coming to Jesus, and His response was to reach out to them in love and give them what they needed. They had only met Him, they didn't have time to prove themselves. They reached out in simple faith and their faith was rewarded. As you stand in faith for the miracle you need, you must have this assurance. God is not looking at you, measuring what you have done to see if you are qualified to receive your request. When you are a Christian, He sees you holy and clean, washed by the precious blood of Jesus. It is through this sacrifice that we are invited to come into the very Holy of Holies to find grace to help in time of need. (Hebrews 4:16) Jesus' sacrifice opened the way for us to come boldly before the throne of grace. We stand before Him holy and clean, righteous in His sight, accepted in the Beloved. We have no fear, only faith in God who loves us so much.

The Bible says that the Father has qualified us to be partakers of the inheritance of the saints in light. (Colossians 1:12) What a glorious promise! We are qualified by the Father Himself to be partakers of this inheritance. If God has qualified us, what more is there to do? It also says that we are given exceeding great and precious promises that by these we may be partakers of the divine nature. (II Peter 1:4) Meditate on that for awhile. By the promises, by the Word of God we are partakers of the divine nature. Not by anything that we have done, but by the blood of the Son we have been redeemed. At that moment we believe the promise of God that declares we are new creatures in Christ. And those promises make us partakers of the nature of God Himself. You are a daughter of the Most High God. You are a woman of faith. You are a woman of God. You are a king and a priest unto God. You have the very nature of God within you.

Jesus said, "I am the vine. You are the branches." (John 15:5) As you look at a vine in a garden, you see that the branch is a natural outgrowth of the vine. It isn't a different color or texture or type of plant – it is the same as the vine. A grapevine produces branches that grow grapes. The branch carries the life force from the vine. In the same way, the Spirit of God flows through us as the children of God. We have been made to be like God! Jesus said that those who come to Him, out of their belly would flow rivers of living water. (John 7:38) He was speaking of the Holy Spirit, the same Spirit that raised Christ from the dead. That Spirit of God, the power of God is in our innermost being, and flows out of us as we walk on this earth. Our bodies are the temple of the Holy Spirit. (I Corinthians 3:16) Glory to God!

So don't think of yourself as being the same as you were. You are a brand new creature. Within you is the very Spirit of God. You are a child of God. You have been adopted into His family. You have been given His very nature. God has declared you justified, righteous and holy in His sight. There is nothing to hold you back. If you believe God, you can reach out and do all that is in your heart because of what Jesus has done for you. Nothing is impossible to him who believes!

You are a woman of faith. You can believe God. You can see miracles happen in your life and the lives of those around you. You can make a difference in this world. Because of what Jesus has done, you can stand before a holy God and know that you are accepted completely, free to walk in newness of life.

❧ CHAPTER 4 ❧
THAT I MAY KNOW HIM

"That I may know Him, and the power of His resur-
rection, and the fellowship of His sufferings, being
made conformable unto His death;"

Philippians 3:10

The most important aspect of this life of faith is to know the
One in whom you believe. Paul prayed, "that I may know
Him..." (Philippians 3:10) Our heart's desire must be to
know God above everything else. When you are born again,
when you realize that God loved you so much, He gave His
only Son for you, you begin a life-long quest of knowing
God intimately. Daily you confide in Him not just your
wish-list of supply that you need, but opening your heart to
Him to grow in a relationship with the living God who
invites you into His presence. You do not have to shrink
back in fear, but as you stand before Him in the robe of
righteousness which He has given you, you can open all your
heart to Him and allow Him free reign in your life.

The Father already knows all about you. He created you! David said in Psalm 139 that while we were still in our mothers' womb God knew us. While we were being formed, God knew every detail of our lives. Jesus assured us that He knows what we need before we ask Him. (Matthew 6:8) He knows us in detail. Jesus said the hairs of our head are numbered! (Matthew 10:30) In the book of Psalms it is recorded that His thoughts toward us are more than can be numbered. (Psalm 139:18) God is thinking about you constantly. And His thoughts toward you are for good and not evil, to give you a future and a hope. (Jeremiah 29:11) We can reach out to Him in faith, with no fear, knowing that God's love has been displayed for us when He sent His only begotten Son to pay the penalty for our sin. "If God is for us, who can be against us? He who did not spare His own Son, but delivered Him up for us all, how shall He not with Him also freely give us all things?" (Romans 8:31-32) We can be confident of the love of the Father God who gave His only Son to bring us into a relationship with Him.

We read the story of the prodigal son and see a picture of the love of the Father. (Luke 15:11-32) Even when one leaves in rebellion, thinking the world has better things to offer, the Father waits patiently, looking daily to see the return of his lost one. That is the love of our Father God, waiting for us to come to our senses and come home; to leave the pig sty of the world and return to the comfort and security and provision of home. I long to know this God more and more intimately.

It is not just a one-way relationship, "what's in it for me." We are to respond to this love by giving our all to Him. There are so many times when I think about the Lord and all that He has done for me, all I can do is offer praises and offer myself in return. I present myself as a living sacrifice to

Him. (Romans 12:1-2) I ask that He use me to bring glory to His name. I live to please Him. I live to honor Him. I live to be used by Him so that others will come to know Him.

As you walk with God in the light of His Word, you will find that life is full of possibilities instead of impossibilities. With God's help, you can do anything! Nothing is impossible to him who believes. All things are possible to him who believes. This is the life of faith, a life of possibilities and dreams come true. The great requirement is that we believe in God and believe in Jesus, His Son. We believe that God so loved the world, so loved me, that He gave His Son, and if He gave His only begotten Son, won't He give me anything else I need?

James says that we have not because we ask not. (James 4:2) Jesus invited us to "ask, and you shall receive." (Matthew 7:7) Faith is relying upon God and His Word. We ask God and believe that He will answer and give us what is needed. We actually hear Him speak to us in our hearts. His "still, small voice" speaks to us throughout the day; directing us, encouraging us, correcting us. Our relationship with God which is built upon faith and His Word becomes a part of us. It is a living, vital strength. As the Bible says, "In Him we live, and move and have our being." (Acts 17:28) This walk of faith is not a stale religious observance or tradition, but a dynamic reality that is as much a part of us as breathing.

This is the primary reason for faith – that we can enjoy the relationship with God that He has forever intended. When He made Adam and Eve, His delight, the crown of creation, He made them for fellowship with Himself. They walked together in the cool of the day, fellowshipping and sharing in

His joy. That has always been God's plan – to have a people, a family. Adam and Eve sinned and man's fellowship with God was broken. But now the way has been made through our faith in Jesus Christ Who has opened the door to the Holy of Holies – so that we can come into the very presence of God. The purpose for faith is not for heaping up treasures on earth, but to know God and His love and His power. Then as we seek God, all the things that are life's necessities will come to us. As we said at the outset, it is faith that pleases God. This faith makes the way for constant communion with the Father. The greatest joy in the life of a Christian is to know God intimately, rejoicing in the peace that passes all understanding when you walk with Him. Worries and concerns of this life are all lifted from our shoulders as we take His yoke upon ourselves and learn of Him. We find rest unto our souls. (Matthew 11:28-30) We are never alone! God is always with us. What a delight to know Him! And when we delight ourselves in the Lord, He gives us the desires of our heart. (Psalms 37:4) Struggle and strife is over. We live in the peace and rest of the Lord Himself.

God has made the way for this relationship through the blood of His Only Son. Don't miss your opportunity to know Him and walk with Him. Throughout the Bible it is recorded that God's love was reaching out to His people, but they did not want Him. They did not want to walk with Him. Even as Jesus, God in the flesh, ministered in Israel, His people did not recognize Him, did not know Him. At the end of His time on earth, Jesus stood looking over Jerusalem and wept. He said, "If you had known. . ." I pray that we will never miss our opportunity to know Him, to truly know Him. Not just know about Him but to know Him intimately, better than anyone else we know.

❧ CHAPTER 5 ❧
FAITH WORKS BY LOVE

"For in Jesus Christ neither circumcision availeth anything, nor uncircumcision; but faith which worketh by love."

Galatians 5:6

The Word of God is excellent in providing definite instructions for living a life that is fruitful, abundant and blessed by God. As we have learned, faith is absolutely necessary in order to be pleasing to God, without it we cannot please Him. Now this verse in the book of Galatians tells us how faith works– faith works by love. Of course we must begin with the love that God has for us, as demonstrated through the gift of His Son. A very familiar verse describes the love that God has for us. John 3:16 says, "For God so loved the world that He gave His only begotten Son, that whosoever believeth upon Him shall not perish, but have everlasting life." God loves us so much that He gave His only Son for us. What a priceless gift! He gave His Son to save us. The Bible further declares,

"Herein is love: not that we loved God but that He first loved us and sent His Son to be the propitiation for our sins." (I John 4:10) God loved us first. He loved us before we could love Him in return. He loved us so much that He watched His only Son die a horrible death at the hand of Roman executioners in order that you and I could be adopted into His family, to become His sons and daughters. The Bible says it pleased the Father to bruise Him. (Isaiah 53:10) God knew that eternal justice would be served as His Son became the complete sacrifice for our sins. This great love saw through the ages to you and me, and provided for our salvation and redemption and adoption as sons and daughters through the gift of His Son. What wonderful love! In fact, the Bible says that God showed His love for us in that while we were yet sinners, Christ died for us. (Romans 5:8) While we were still unthankful, unholy, lost in sin, following the wants and whims of our flesh, Jesus suffered untold agony for us so that one day we would be able to become sons and daughters of the Most High God. We live in an "I'll scratch your back if you'll scratch mine" world. People rarely give just for the joy of giving. But God so loved that He gave. He gave knowing that many would scoff at Him and reject His gift. But He also knew that you and I would come to Him and love Him in return and give our lives to Him, spending every moment seeking to bring honor to His name.

This kind of love is life-giving and ennobling and humbling all at once. To think that the King of the universe would take the form of human flesh and endure life in this world limited by time and space, then beyond that allow Himself to become the sacrifice for sin which He did not commit– all for the love He has for you and me.

Hebrews 12:2 encourages us to look unto Jesus the author and finisher of our faith; who for the joy that was set before him endured he cross, despising the shame, and is set down at the right hand of the throne of God." What joy was set before Him? It was the joy of realizing the fulfillment of the plan of the Father, to redeem mankind to Himself, the joy of seeing you and me in His Kingdom as members of His family, able to enjoy eternity together. The Bible declares that Jesus came to seek and to save that which was lost. We were lost! He came to seek us out, to save us from our sin.

So in this walk of faith, we find great strength and peace in knowing this wonderful love. In His love, the Father saw you and knew you and desired that you would be His, living forever with Him in the wonderful Kingdom He has prepared for you. He planned to take care of you forever, filling you with His fullness and giving you a special place in His kingdom. Even though we were in sin and without God, He still loved us and gave His Only Son for us. Such love is beyond description. Paul said in Ephesians 3:17-21, that Christ dwells in our hearts by faith and that we must be rooted and grounded in this love. This love is our foundation. When we know this love, we are stable throughout the course of life. When we know the lengths to which the Father would go for us, any difficulty or trouble becomes miniscule when compared to the strength that we find in that love. In this passage, Paul goes on to pray that we would be able to comprehend with all saints what is its breadth, and length, and depth and height and to know the love of Christ which passes knowledge, to be filled with all the fullness of God. The more you grow in the Lord, the more you realize that His love can carry you and surround you and fill you and lift you up in this life. You live each day in awe of this amazing reality– Jesus loves me! If He loves me, He will take care of me. He will protect me. He will provide for me. He will help me. In fact, Romans 8:37-39 says that nothing, nothing can separate us from this love. "For I am persuaded, that neither death, nor life, nor angels, nor principalities, nor powers, nor things present, nor things to come, nor height, nor depth, nor any other creature, shall be able to separate us from the love of God which is in Christ Jesus our Lord." There is nothing in all creation that can separate you from His wonderful love, the love which is our abiding place throughout eternity. This relationship of love is the one that Jesus enjoys with the Father, and wants us to enjoy with Him. John 15:9 says, "As the Father hath loved me, so have I loved you: continue ye in my love." We are to continue, to abide, to remain in this resting place of love, regardless of the storms that may be raging around us. In his first letter, John describes God with this one word: love. God is love. So in knowing God, you must know that He loves you. He can't help loving you. And in this great assurance of His love, you can walk on in life, knowing that there is absolutely nothing that can take that love away from you or hinder its power in your life.

One of the chief lies of the enemy is to use circumstances to persuade us that God doesn't love us. When we encounter something difficult, or face the attack of the enemy, the devil tries to tell us that God must not love us any more. "If God loves me, why is this happening to me?" We have an enemy. He is the one who comes to kill, steal and destroy. After he has attacked you, he throws that question in your mind: why? There could be many different answers to that question, but the bottom line is that the devil hates you and wants to see you turn away from God. If we are rooted and grounded in God's love, and in His Word, we know that through any difficulty we are more than conquerors. His love will carry us through any storm. His love will strengthen us to face any trial or trouble. There is absolutely nothing that can separate us from that love.

Even when we have blown it, and walked away following our own desires, God is like the father of the prodigal son, watching for our return. Jesus gave us this wonderful story to reveal to us the unconditional love of the Father. (Luke 15:11-32) The prodigal son took his inheritance, all the blessings that came from his relationship with his father, and squandered them on the pleasures that this life has to offer. After going through all his money, he found himself with the pigs. The Bible says that the son "came to himself" and realized that even his father's hired hands didn't have it as bad as he did. He was certain he had forfeited all privileges of sonship, but hoped his father would hire him as a common laborer. What a surprise to arrive at home to find his father waiting for him with a robe and ring and shoes – restoring his full standing as a son. He even threw a party in honor of his son's return! This is the love the Father God has for you and me. Even when we make mistakes, going after our own game plan instead of His, He is still waiting for us to return to Him, pick up where we left off and get back on track. The Bible says His mercy endures forever! Now, as the Bible says, we do not frustrate His wonderful grace; but we know that God forgives. His mercies are new every morning. His grace is sufficient for us. We are not perfect, we all make mistakes. But we are confident that His love never fails. Nothing in this life, nothing in creation, no power or principality can keep us from that love. In this walk of faith we must be rooted in that blessed assurance, that God loves me no matter what. We can run into those open arms, in the very throne room of mercy and find grace to help in time of need. What love! This love is the bedrock. This love is the foundation. Faith works by this wonderful love!

Now, being filled with the love of God is immersing yourself in a heavenly river of joy and peace. Leaning on Him, trusting Him in every situation provides the source of peace and strength to walk in victory. But this wonderful love is not meant for us to keep for ourselves. When we are filled with His love and fullness, we can't help but share it with the world around us. This love that God pours out upon us isn't just for us, to make us feel good. This love is to fill us to overflowing to a lost and dying world, a world filled with heartache and need. The Bible says that Jesus came to seek and to save that which was lost. (Luke 19:10) He came to find us, to save us and to bring us into His kingdom. When we have received such life-transforming love, how can we keep it to ourselves? I John 4:7-11 tells us to love one another. It says that everyone who loves is born of God and knows God. Conversely, if you don't love you don't know God because God is love. Verse 11 says that if God so loved us, we also ought to love one another. It is very simple. If you are born again, you have the Spirit of God on the inside of you. That Spirit is love. That Spirit of love gives you the compassion and the ability to love the world around you. Paul wrote that the love of Christ constrained him to reach out to the lost, facing intense persecution, yet continuing in the ministry to which he had been called. He couldn't help it. The love of Christ was a powerful force on the inside of him that gave him the will and the strength to carry out the plan and purpose of God in reaching out to the world around him.

Jesus gave us this commandment, that we should love one another as He has loved us. (John 15:12) In other words, out of His love for us and the example of His life, we are to love those around us. This is not an easy task, but because we have the very nature of God on the inside of us, we are able to follow this command and love those who may be unlovely. We are able to reach out to those who have never known the love of God. We are able to stand in the face of opposition and persecution and still love. Just as Jesus cried out from the cross on behalf of the very ones who had driven the nails in IIis hands and feet, "Father, forgive them, for they know not what they do;" we have that same love on the inside of us. We have the love that can forgive again and again, having compassion on those who have hurt us. We can reach out to those who don't know God and need His saving grace.

Our faith is not meant just for ourselves, to receive blessings and all that we need from God. Our faith is moved by love to reach out to get a miracle for someone else. I don't know about you, but I remember my life before I knew God in His fullness. I didn't know about miracles. I didn't know that God would supply my need. I didn't know that I could come to Him for impossible situations in my life and see them change right in front of me. Now that I know the power of God and His ability to act in my life, I want to tell others of His fullness and His wonderful love for you and me. My faith works by love to reach out to the world around me. This faith is too marvelous to keep to myself. The love of God compels me to share this Good News with the world around me.

Jesus said in His instructions to His disciples, "Freely you have received, freely give." When you have received this marvelous new life in Christ and a position in His Kingdom, a place in His family; it is too much to keep for yourself. When you realize your authority as a child of God you want to use that authority to help others who don't know Jesus. When Jesus sent out His disciples, He said they were to "Heal the sick, cleanse the lepers, raise the dead, cast out devils. Freely you have received, freely give." (Matthew 10:8) This life of faith is to be used on behalf of a hurting world. In the last chapter of Mark, Jesus said there would be signs following those who believe. They would lay hands on the sick and they would recover. This comes as an overflow of your relationship with God. You are filled with His love and compassion, and so when you see someone in pain or in need, you reach out your hand to heal and to bless, to give and to help. This life of faith isn't just for the accumulation of things for yourself, but as God pronounced over Abraham's life, you are blessed to be a blessing. (Genesis 12:2) We have our needs supplied and more, so that we can give to those who are in want. We have come to know the Lord as our Shepherd, therefore we do not want. But there are those who do not know Him. God uses us to bring provision to them to demonstrate His love for them. This is a great testimony to the love of the Lord who uses us to bring the Good News in many practical ways; not only in teaching and preaching, but in giving and healing and praying. Through His love we reach out to a lost world, that they might come to know this wonderful Jesus and the Almighty Father God who can meet their every need.

✧ CHAPTER 6 ✧
WALK BY THE SPIRIT

"For as many as are led by the Spirit of God, they are the sons of God."

Romans 8:14

Walking by faith requires that you walk according to the Spirit, and not according to the flesh – the natural man. You must learn to listen to that still small voice guiding you and directing you. Walking by faith requires that we believe in Someone we have not seen with our natural eyes, but by the Spirit we trust completely. Romans 8:14 declares, all who are led by the Spirit of God are sons of God. Jesus said, God is Spirit and those who worship Him must worship Him in Spirit and in truth. (John 4:24) Many people make the mistake of trying to understand God with their heads, and He can only be known in your heart! For example, when you consider that He is "I Am". Your mind wants to know – when did He begin? He didn't begin – He Is! He has always been and always will be. Your mind cannot understand that concept. But your heart says "Amen! That's my Father!"

One of the greatest battles in walking by faith is the battle of the mind. Your mind will tell you that it doesn't make sense to walk with God, to obey His Word. For example, in the area of finances the Bible instructs us to give to God first. Honor Him with the first fruits of all your increase – then your barns will be filled with plenty and your vats will burst forth with new wine. (Proverbs 3:9-10) Your mind tells you, "Be careful! You should figure out your budget first to see if you have enough to give. Times are tough. You need to save for the future. All that preacher wants is your money, anyway." But the Word of God commands that we honor God by giving to Him first. Then we will have increase. "Give, and it shall be given unto you; pressed down, shaken together and running over shall men give unto your bosom. For with the same measure you mete withal it shall be measured unto you again." (Luke 6:38) By faith, believing God at His Word, we give first and then we will be blessed.

A wonderful example of this is in the Old Testament in the ministry of Elijah. (I Kings 17:8-16) There was a famine in the land, and Elijah approached a woman for something to eat. She told him she was destitute, preparing her last meal for herself and her son. Elijah, as a prophet of God, told her to prepare a cake for him first, then feed her family. Can you imagine? This woman and her son were on the brink of starvation and the prophet of God asked her to feed him first. She found faith in her heart to believe the prophet, and fed him first, then herself and her son. In that act of faith – giving to God first – the woman was rewarded with a never-ending supply of meal and oil. No matter how much she used in cooking, each time she went to the barrel of meal there was more meal! Every time she went to the jar of oil there was more oil! God will bless you and reward you and provide for you when you follow His Word. I don't know what her thoughts were as she prepared that cake for the prophet, but if she was like the rest of us, her mind was probably screaming "What are you doing? This is your last bit of food, and you are giving it away! You are crazy!" I'm glad she didn't follow the reasoning of her mind, but followed the voice of God through the prophet who brought God's blessing of never-ending supply.

In fact, the Bible says that the reasoning of the mind of the flesh is enmity against God. (Romans 8:7) The natural man, the flesh, is hostile to God. It is crucial to your walk with the Lord that you learn to walk by the Spirit and not by natural reasoning. God speaks to you through your spirit, and you must learn to listen for His voice. He will guide you, direct you and show you things to come. (John 16:13) But your mind will continually question what God says, and the enemy will sow doubt in your mind to try to persuade you to stop following God and believing what He says. Instead, you must walk by the Spirit and the Word of God. It doesn't always make "sense" to follow the Word of the Lord, as you can see from the example in the life of Elijah. That is why you must learn to follow the Spirit. You will miss the blessing of God and His miracles if you continue to walk according to your natural reasoning. God is Spirit. God is supernatural, not natural. As His child, as a daughter of God, you are created in His image. You were made to walk in the supernatural. Romans 8:14-15 says that all who are led by the Spirit of God, they are sons of God. The spirit we have been given is not the spirit of the world, bringing us into the bondage of fear, but the spirit of adoption whereby we cry Abba, Father. We walk by the Spirit because we are sons (daughters) of God. The supernatural is our way of life.

It is a new way of living, different from others around you who don't know God in His fullness.

People who are trying to walk with God in the flesh, in the natural realm, look for results instead of focusing on God and simply standing on His Word. The world has a saying, "Seeing is believing." The believer who is walking by faith and walking in the Spirit knows that "Believing is seeing." Jesus said, "If you believe, all things are possible to him that believes." (Mark 9:23) He also said, "If you believe, you will see the glory of God." (John 11:40) If you believe – you will see, just like our Father God who began with emptiness and created the universe. This is very important to understand. When you are walking by faith, you must learn to look beyond the physical, natural world around you. Some people try to walk by faith, try to stand on the Word of God and when it doesn't happen in their time frame, or the way they envisioned; they get upset with God. They begin to blame God for the lack of results, instead of trusting God for the results to come. It is a battle, and you must be prepared to stand and fight! Don't let the enemy defeat you in this area. Stand strong and wait upon the Lord. He will never fail you!

The Bible says if we live in the Spirit, let us walk in the Spirit. (Galatians 5:25-26) Walking in the Spirit means that we allow the Spirit to direct us, rather than reasoning our way through life. Proverbs 3:5-6 says we must trust in the Lord with all our heart, and lean not on our own understanding. In all our ways acknowledge Him, and He shall direct our paths. We are used to making our own way. There are those who are "self-made successes." We pride ourselves on pulling ourselves up by our own bootstraps. And there is that song, "I did it my way." Now, God has given us talent and abilities and intelligence. I'm not suggesting that you set all that aside and simply wait for God to do it. But we must continually look to the Lord for guidance and direction. He can lead us in ways of which we have no natural knowledge. We will find true fulfillment in life when we walk in the Spirit, not in the flesh.

Let's look at an example from the life of David. He had been anointed as king of Israel by the prophet Samuel. God made a way for him to attend Saul as a psalmist, and David became a mighty warrior. David's great successes in battle made Saul jealous, and David literally had to run for his life. David was in the wilderness for several years, until Saul was killed in battle. Even after Saul was killed in battle, and David knew he had already been anointed king of Israel, David asked the Lord, "Should I go up to the children of Israel? Where?" (II Samuel 2:1) David didn't presume that the circumstances dictated his actions, he inquired of the Lord. He waited for the Lord's direction. We must not presume to evaluate circumstances in our own reasoning. We must constantly seek the Lord and be open and waiting for His direction.

I remember an occasion several years ago, when my husband and I were first starting in the ministry. We were believing God for every penny, and there weren't many extra pennies! One night we went grocery shopping and my husband picked up a bag of dog food. Now we didn't even own a dog, and this was top of the line dog food. I asked him why he was buying the dog food, and he said he just felt impressed to buy it for this young man we had been witnessing to who had a dog. We stopped at the man's apartment and left the dog food at the door. A few days later, he shared with us that he had been thinking about our witnessing. He was so discouraged, had no money, and his dog was out of food. He prayed a simple prayer and said, "God, I don't know how to pray, but please send me some food for my dog." Then he came home and there was the food right on his doorstep. He gave his life to the Lord that day! Hallelujah! The Lord knows how to direct us to touch the lives of others for His Kingdom! This is walking in the Spirit, receiving direction and guidance from the Lord. This life of faith isn't all about me – it's all about Him and the lost world that He came to seek and to save.

❧ CHAPTER 7 ❧
THE SHUNAMMITE WOMAN

"Women received their dead raised to life again . . ."

Hebrews 11:35

One of my favorite stories in the Bible concerns a distinguished lady who believed the prophet and received several miracles. We read her testimony in II Kings 4:8-37. The woman was a Shunammite woman, the Bible says she was a "notable woman." She and her husband took care of the man of God, the prophet Elisha, on his journey through their area. Every time he passed that way, they invited him for dinner. As time went on, she felt prompted to build a room for him in their home so that he would have a place to stay. She responded to that prompting in obedience. When the prophet asked what she would like in return for her generous hospitality, she replied that she didn't want anything. The prophet asked if she would like a word of favor spoken to the king or to the general on her behalf, but she responded that she had a position among her own people. But Gehazi, the prophet's assistant, noticed that the couple was childless. He suggested that perhaps she would like a son. Anyone who has been through the pain of barrenness knows that sometimes there comes a point when you give up all hope and simply resign yourself to the fact that you are not going to have a family. So when the prophet called to her and declared that she would have a son the next year, she replied, "No, my lord. Man of God, do not lie to your maidservant!" She didn't want to even hope that her condition could change and that she would be a mother. But the word of the Lord came to pass and she had a son. The child grew, then one day as he was helping his father in the field, his head began to hurt and he went in to his mother. She held him, soothing him and comforting him the best she could but he died in her arms. She laid the body of her son on the bed of the prophet in the room they had prepared for him and went to find the man of God. Despite her great grief, she embarked on a journey of faith. When she told her husband where she was going, she didn't tell him that their only son was dead. She didn't cry out to him in bitterness of soul. She simply declared, "It is well." Now that is a woman of faith! Just think, her only son was lying dead in the prophet's room and she said, "It is well." She went with provision and offerings to find the man of God and to bring him back. She withheld her anguish until she reached the man of God. Even as she was approaching, when Gehazi went to meet her and inquire of her state and that of her husband and child, she responded that all was well. Not until she was face to face with the man of God, in grief and disappointment clinging to his feet, did she pour out her anguish. "Did I ask a son of my lord? Did I not say, 'Do not deceive me.'" The prophet sent Gehazi with his staff to lay it on the child, but the Shunammite woman declared her singleness of faith,

"As the Lord lives, and as your soul lives, I will not leave you." She was determined to have a miracle from the Lord. She was not going to let the prophet go until he ministered to her son. That is the single-hearted tenacity required to walk by faith. You believe God for a miracle and you don't let go until you get one! So the prophet immediately went to her home where he laid down on the bed on top of the cold body of her dead son, and the boy was raised up. This notable lady's faith triumphed in the midst of grief and loss, and she received her son back to life again. How did she receive the miracle? She kept her heart fastened on the hope of life in her son. She kept the confession of her mouth in line with the faith in her heart. When her husband asked, she answered, "It is well." When Gehazi asked, she answered, "It is well." When people around us ask, we can answer, "It is well."

I want you to see from this story that as women of God, we can take a stand of faith. This Shunammite woman who received the miracle of a child, and then received that child raised from the dead, believed that "It is well." And that's what she received. The Bible seems to indicate that this was a stand of faith she made alone. Her husband was left in the field, not knowing the tragedy that had just occurred. She stood in faith for her son to be given back to her from the dead. If your husband doesn't know God, or if his faith is not strong in an area, don't sit back and let the devil run all over your life. Stand up and declare the Word of the Lord and see the reward of your faith. If no one else believes – you can believe! If no one else knows how to stand on the Word– you can stand on the Word. Many of God's children do not experience all that God has for them because they shy away, not wanting to step out in faith for themselves. Wives are often tempted to hang back instead of going on in God, because they are waiting for their mates to take the first step. I am not proposing that you push ahead of your husband in an attitude of competition, but that you go on with God in faith, believing His Word and trusting what He has told you. Stand in faith for your family, your home, your church, your business. God has great things for those who will trust Him.

The Word of God is clear that God is no respecter of persons. He has made the way for our salvation. The Bible says it is for everyone who believes (Romans 1:16). One word for salvation is the Greek word "sozo" which means life in its fullness, the God kind of life. He wants all of His children, male and female, to walk in the abundant life He has promised us.

"For you are all sons of God through faith in Christ Jesus. For as many of you as were baptized into Christ have put on Christ. There is neither Jew nor Greek, there is neither slave nor free, there is neither male nor female; for you are all one in Christ Jesus. And if you are Christ's, then you are Abraham's seed, and heirs according to the promise." (Galatians 3:26-29)

As a woman of God, you are an heir of God according to the promise. You inherit the Kingdom that the Father has prepared for you. Jesus said, "Do not fear, little flock, for it is your Father's good pleasure to give you the Kingdom." (Luke 12:32) It is your Father's good pleasure. God is your Father. When Jesus gave us the model prayer, He prayed, "Our Father." Daughter of God, you can call upon your Father in faith, knowing that He has the miracle you need and is glad to give it to you. Don't hold back or draw back for anyone or anything. Believe God and allow His Spirit to move in your life!

The prophet Joel declared, and Peter quotes in Acts 2:17-18, "And it shall come to pass in the last days, says God, that I will pour out of My Spirit on all flesh; your sons and your daughters shall prophesy, your young men shall see visions, your old men shall dream dreams. And on My menservants and on My maidservants I will pour out My Spirit in those days; and they shall prophesy." Daughters shall prophesy, the maidservants of the Lord shall prophesy out of the fullness of the Holy Spirit which has been poured out. Peter declared on the day of Pentecost – this is the fulfillment of the prophecy given to Joel. The Spirit has been poured out upon all flesh. Daughters of God, move in the Holy Spirit. Go deeper in the things of God. Walk by faith which is pleasing to God, and see what He will do with you in this wonderful, abundant life. Don't hold back or quench the Holy Spirit, but move in faith and in obedience to God.

Sometimes I wonder if we have forgotten that we will all stand before God to give an answer to Him for this life He has given us. Jesus said we would even answer for every idle word that we have spoken, including the murmuring under our breath that we thought no one would hear. We will see Jesus. We will look into that glorious face. We will answer for what we have done with the gifts He has given us in this life. Jesus taught us in the parable of the talents that He expects us to do something with the gifts we have been given. We are to bear fruit that is pleasing to God. And we will have to give an account of our stewardship. Women of God, don't let excuses hold you back from fulfilling God's plan and purpose for your life. Don't let the gifts within you lie dormant, but rise up and move on in faith to see the glory of God displayed as you obey Him. God is watching over His Word to perform it for you! (Jeremiah 1:12)

✎ CHAPTER 8 ✍
THE EXAMPLE OF SARAH

*"By faith Sarah herself also received strength to conceive
seed, and she bore a child when she was past the age,
because she judged Him faithful who had promised."*

Hebrews 11:11

We recall in the account of Abraham and Sarah that they
were a barren couple and "well advanced in years." When the
Lord promised them a son, the Bible says that Sarah
laughed. She giggled – nervously, in anticipation, with
delight? But despite her initial reaction, Hebrews records
that Sarah had faith. It was by that faith that she received
strength to conceive seed. All natural hope for children was
gone. But out of her impossibility, faith rose in her heart to
believe the Word of the Lord. She received strength, ability
in her body to conceive and she gave birth to the son of
promise – Isaac. Remember, Sarah was ninety years old
when Isaac was born. She had gone through life bearing the
stigma of barrenness. In her desire to have children, she gave
Hagar, her handmaid, to Abraham to produce a child and

Ishmael was born. But God said, "No, Sarah will have a son." What a wonderful truth! Even when we blow it, and connive and conspire to figure out how to make things happen, God is still true to His promise. Notice how Hebrews 11:11 says that "she judged Him faithful who had promised." God is faithful to His Word. He watches over His Word to perform it. His Word does not return to Him void. It accomplishes its purpose. When mixed with faith, the Word brings results in our lives because God is faithful. Sarah received strength, ability, in her ninety-year-old body to have a child and Isaac, the son of promise, was born!

In I Peter 3, the Lord instructs us to look at the example of Sarah as a submissive wife. She demonstrated her faith when she followed Abraham from their home in Ur to move to an unknown location at God's direction. We can put ourselves in her place as she went through the house, packing everything and preparing for a journey to – where? Imagine how she felt, leaving everything familiar to follow her husband who said he had a word from God. Now that's faith! Remember, Abraham was a wealthy man. He and Sarah lived in a beautiful home. Can you put yourself in her place as she is walking through the house for the last time, savoring the memories and then closing the door to head out to a place that God would show them?

Then, along the way, Abraham instructed Sarah to declare that she was his sister and omit the fact that she was his wife. (She was Abraham's half sister. They had the same father but different mothers.) Sarah was a beautiful woman, even in her advanced age, and Abraham was afraid for his life. Sarah obeyed Abraham and was promptly put in a harem where she, along with all the other ladies, awaited the king's summons. Not once, but TWICE, God protected her and did not allow the king to call. And when the truth was discovered, the kings sent Abraham and Sarah on their way loaded down with gifts. God blessed Sarah's obedience, her faith, and her strength alongside her husband Abraham.

The first such incident is recorded in Genesis 12 where Abraham and Sarah traveled to Egypt. Verse 15 records, "The princes of Pharaoh also saw her and commended her to Pharaoh, and the woman was taken to Pharaoh's house." This must have been quite a dilemma for Sarah. The Bible goes on to say that "he (Pharaoh) treated Abram well for her sake." Because of Sarah, Abram was blessed. "He had sheep, oxen, male donkeys, male and female servants, female donkeys, and camels." Abraham was treated like a visiting dignitary, loaded down with provision and increased in wealth because Sarah obeyed by declaring that she was his sister. At the same time, God protected Sarah. Beginning with verse 17, "But the Lord plagued Pharaoh and his house with great plagues because of Sarai, Abram's wife. And Pharaoh called Abram and said, 'What is this you have done to me? Why did you not tell me that she was your wife? Why did you say, "She is my sister"? I might have taken her as my wife. Now therefore, here is your wife, take her and go your way.'" God "plagued Pharaoh with great plagues because of Sarai, Abram's wife." The pharaoh was plagued by God while Sarah was in his house. God protected Sarah. She wasn't taken as a wife but honored as a guest. Her husband was showered with gifts of livestock and servants. And when the truth was discovered, they were sent on their way with all they had.

As they continued on their travels, they came to Gerar where Abimelech was king. (Genesis 20) The same thing happened to Sarah. She declared that she was Abraham's sister and was taken into the king's house. God spoke to Abimelech in a dream, revealing the truth to him. King Abimelech sent for Abraham, gave him back his wife along with "sheep, oxen and male and female servants". Again, God protected Sarah. She was not called upon by the king during her stay in the palace. Not only that, no other woman in the house conceived children while Sarah was there, until Abraham prayed for them. As a special vindication for Sarah, Abraham was given 1000 pieces of silver, a rather handsome sum! Abimelech declared, "Indeed this vindicates you before all who are with you and before everybody."

Of course, we can't know how Sarah was feeling as she went not once but twice into the palace of a king. I can only imagine it was a difficult place to be. It must have been nice to be pampered and petted in the palace, but certainly not peaceful when she knew all the while that she was a married woman and her husband was camped outside! If she was anything like women today, I'm sure her thoughts were racing between fear of the situation, blaming Abraham for getting her into this mess AGAIN, and trying to relax and enjoy the privileges of palace life.

I Peter 3:6 says, "as Sarah obeyed Abraham, calling him lord, whose daughters you are if you do good and are not afraid with any terror." We have seen that Sarah's obedience brought the blessing of God upon herself and her husband. As she left the comforts of home to follow her husband to the land of promise, as she told foreign officials that she was Abraham's sister, as she meekly endured the rigors of life on the road in a tent or the pleasures of a palace, Sarah's submission to Abraham earned her financial rewards and favor. She is our example. . . "whose daughters you are if you do good and are not afraid with any terror." It takes faith to do good –

- Obeying your husband as he is following God's leading when you don't see it
- Obeying your husband when the consequences are dubious
- Obeying your husband again, in the same situation.

That takes faith! In this verse from I Peter, it says that we are to do good with no fear. We stand strong in the Lord, resisting the enemy, remembering that God hasn't given us a spirit of fear, but of power and of love and of a sound mind. (II Timothy 1:7) We are to obey in this manner, doing good with no fear of the consequences because we know that God will bless us, God will protect us, as we follow the His Word.

Submission in this manner keeps you in the right place for God's work to be done in your life. Although we may not fully understand, we may be fighting off doubts about the outcome, we may wonder where this path will lead – the strength of faith in a woman of God who is submitted to God and to the authorities in her life brings unequaled blessing.

Before we leave the example of Sarah, I want to emphasize the attitude of submission. We can say, "Yes, dear," with our mouths and be raging in our hearts. That's where the "meek and quiet spirit" comes in. We can submit our hearts and minds to the Lord, putting away anger, knowing that Jesus is Lord. Ephesians 5:22 says, "Wives, be subject to your own husbands as to the Lord." When we submit ourselves as unto Jesus, knowing that He is Lord in the situation, we can be confident in the outcome. He will protect us, keep us, provide for us; even though the decision we are following may be questionable. Just as He protected Sarah, He will protect us. This is another arena of faith! Let faith rise in your heart, despite the situation or the conflict. When your heart reaches out to God in faith, He always answers. Remember, God is in charge! We submit to our husbands as to the Lord. Jesus is Lord of your life, and He will move in the present circumstances to take care of you. We must believe Him at His Word.

This matter of submission is very important when it comes to following God. We cannot pick and choose the scriptures we like and only obey them, we must obey God in everything. If you are a married woman, you are to be submissive to your husband with no complaining. Now this flies in the face of current culture. Many married couples simply live in the same house, with no sense of unity or dependence on one another. They each have their own occupation, hobbies, interests, friends. They only interact when necessary to handle the responsibilities of life. God wants more for us. He wants a union that is full of life and full of love and full of His presence. This comes when we honor God and His Word, which includes being submissive to our husbands. The Bible says wives, submit to your husbands. Treat him with respect and honor. Do this as unto the Lord, knowing that it is pleasing to God. And the attitude with which we are to submit is described in I Peter 3:4. Peter is encouraging women not to merely dress up and look good outwardly, but to take thought of the inner woman, your inner beauty. He says to let our beauty be of the hidden person of the heart, which is not corruptible, a gentle and peaceful spirit, which is in the sight of God of great price. God values the radiance of the inner woman, namely a gentle and peaceful spirit. Not one that is worried and upset and nervous or nagging or complaining, but one that is gentle and peaceful, meek and quiet. This takes faith! You must continually look to the Lord, knowing that He is taking care of you regardless of the circumstances or your husband's decisions. God will take care of you! We don't have to nag or get upset or pout or throw a temper tantrum. God will take care of us! We look to Jesus, the Author and Finisher of our faith. His Word to us is true and He watches over His Word to perform it in our lives. His promises to us are yes and in Him amen!

Now, submission is not a demeaning action, but one of strength and honor and obedience. In the government of the family, the husband is the head of the home and the wife is his helper. This does not mean that the wife is any less of a person or that she holds a lower place in the kingdom of God, this simply means that in the family the husband has the final say. We must realize that this submission to our husbands is designed by God to make the family unit a peaceful one. When there is a disagreement about the next step to take, the husband has the final say. Rather than tear the family apart, the wife is to yield to her husband and trust God for the outcome. As you submit in this manner, as I have said before, as to the Lord, you allow God to work in your husband's life to bring direction and correction. Let me say it again, God will take care of you! God, the perfect One, knows how the family unit will work the best and He has given us this order in His Word. Again, it doesn't mean that the woman is any less of a person or that her "rights" are taken away. It simply means that in the family unit, the husband is the head and the wife is to be submissive under him, a support and help to him. When we understand that this is the biblical pattern for the home, we can yield to our husbands and know that ultimately, God is in control!

As a woman our natural tendency is to "fix it." We want to fix the problem and make everything right. Sometimes we can do that. But we must always look to the Lord for His guidance and direction. We must trust Him when it is beyond our ability to make things right. We must not give in to the habit of nagging and yelling or complaining, but draw upon the power of the Holy Spirit to stay peaceful and calm. Remember what we have been learning, we are daughters of the Most High God. We have His nature. We can go through any storm or turmoil in the same peace and calm that allowed Jesus to fall asleep in the boat in the middle of a violent storm. As we remain stable in our faith, we can submit to our husbands and stay in an attitude of peace throughout the difficulties of life. Don't take matters into your own hands. Leave them in the hands of God!

✎ CHAPTER 9 ✎
WATCH YOUR WORDS

Death and life are in the power of the tongue, and they that love it shall eat the fruit thereof."

Proverbs 18:21

"Set a guard over my mouth." (Psalm 141:3) As David prayed this prayer, we need to say it with him. "Set a guard over my mouth." Now women have the reputation for being people of many words. I know all of us don't fit that stereotype, nevertheless, everyone must watch the words they say. This is especially important in the life of faith. The Bible declares that "death and life are in the power of the tongue and they that love it shall eat the fruit thereof." (Proverbs 18:21) In other words, what you say determines the outcome of life for you. There is great power in the words you speak. You can use that power for good or for evil, for death or for life.

Words have creative power. Hebrews tells us that by faith we believe that the worlds were framed by the Word of God. (Hebrews 11:3) Genesis records the creation of the earth. In the beginning, there was nothing, emptiness, void. In the midst of nothingness, in the vast empty space God's voice rang out, "Let there be light" and there was light! His Word created light out of an empty void. Then in His mighty power he separated and named these lights – the sun to rule the day and the moon and stars to rule the night. He began with nothing and simply by the power of His Word commanding light to come forth – there was light! The rest of the world; the water, the dry land, vegetation, animal life were all created by that same power – the Word of God. As His dear children, we have been given this power of the spoken word. It is an awesome and humbling realization to know that the words that I speak have a force in this world. Jesus instructed His disciples to realize that their prayers were not to be "vain repetitions", just saying words, but realizing that the words they spoke were full of power and authority. He said, "Have faith in God. For assuredly I say to you, whoever says to this mountain, 'Be removed and be cast into the sea,' and does not doubt in his heart, but believes that those things he says will be done, he will have whatever he says. Therefore I say to you, whatever things you ask when you pray, believe that you receive them and you will have them." (Mark 11:22-24) Whatever the mountain may be, a mountain of loneliness, a mountain of bills, a mountain of hurt and heartache and disappointment, a mountain of illness; whatever the mountain is that you are facing God says you can speak to that mountain and it will move! With faith in our hearts, believing that what we say will come to pass, we can speak to that mountain! We are not to simply ask for strength to endure, but we are to use the power and authority given us as His children to see the circumstances change in our lives. Nothing is impossible with God! But if we are constantly speaking death and not life – we will have that negative power at work, rather than the power of God. Death and life are in the power of the tongue. If you stand and talk about how big that mountain is, how hard that mountain is, cry out and ask God why there is a mountain there, beg God to do something about that mountain – what will happen? The mountain will stay there, big and bad as ever. You can say, "Well, God gave me this mountain in my life so He must be teaching me something. I don't know what I ever did that was so bad that I deserve to have this mountain in my life. But I'll just ask God to give me strength to endure this mountain." And every day you can get up and live with that mountain. OR one day you can get up and say, "You know I'm tired of looking at this mountain. I command you to move!" And it will obey you! There is power in the word that you speak. It is up to you! You can spend your life talking about the mountain, worrying about the mountain, or you can act on the Word of God and command the mountain to move! And it shall obey you!

The Bible warns us about the idle use of words that we speak, words that are not put to use in speaking faith to the circumstances of life. Jesus said that we will have to give account for every idle word we speak. (Matthew 12:36) That word "idle" means unproductive. We are to speak words that produce, words that bring results. The book of Proverbs describes women who are nagging and fretful as being extremely difficult to live with. They are likened to a dripping faucet. In fact, Solomon says that it's better to live on the rooftop than to live in the house with a contentious, nagging woman! (Proverbs 21:9) Then he goes on to say it's better to live in the desert than with a contentious woman! (Proverbs 21:19) We all know what nagging is: rehearsing the same problem again and again and again. Stop nagging about the problem, instead speak the Word of God to the problem so that God can work to change it. Nagging words are idle words. They are unproductive. What good does it do to go over the problem again and again? Give it to God! Confess His Word! That brings God's power into the situation, which can bring about the answer. We must discipline our mouths so that we speak those things which give grace to the hearers. (Ephesians 4:29) Instead of nagging people around you, speak encouraging words to them, words that minister grace – God's ability. The power of God is released as you speak His Word. Then the nagging stops! God's power is at work! Hallelujah!

This requires more than willpower. It requires a change in your heart. Jesus said out of the abundance of the heart, the mouth speaks. An evil man out of the evil treasure in his heart brings forth evil things and a good man out of the good treasure in his heart brings forth good things. (Matthew 12:34-35) Therefore you must fill your heart with good things – the Word of God and the knowledge of God – so that that is what comes out of your mouth! For example, when that unexpected bill arrives, what is the first thing out of your mouth? Are you ranting and raving about how unfair life is? How are we going to pay this? Who spent this money? Or do you have the good treasure of the Word of God in your heart so that the first thing you speak is, "My Father knows the things I need before I ask Him. My God shall supply all my need according to His riches in glory by Christ Jesus." This is the life of faith. This is reality. It is not living in some bubble, oblivious to life's problems and complexities. But as you are filled with the Word of God and walk with Him daily, His Word flows through you to bring miracles in your life. This is the life abundant that

Jesus came to give us; a life that would be full of hope and possibility instead of discouragement and despair. As we have learned thus far, it begins with a change in your life – a brand new you that continues to grow in the knowledge of God as you read His Word and walk by it each and every day. It is so simple!

WORDS AT HOME

The place where the rubber meets the road is in our home. Many people look at the home as the place where we can let down our hair and relax and let it all hang out. Home should be a welcoming, comfortable place but we are still Christians at home! At home we can do much damage with speaking wrong words. It seems that some Christians think they can be one way out in the world, and when they get home they can let it loose and nobody will know. Let me remind you that God hears, God sees what goes on behind closed doors. You can't raise your hands and sing hallelujah in church and go home and yell and curse and think that God hears only your praise. He hears what you say to your family, and you will be held accountable for it. You must speak the Word of God at home. Home should be the place of love and nurture where we can learn the things of God and the life of faith as we see it lived before us. This Bible that we believe in is not just for church, it is for everyday life, especially life at home. What do you say in your home? What words do you release into the atmosphere of your home? What words do you use toward your spouse or children? The Bible warns us to let no corrupt communication proceed out of our mouth, but only that which is good for the use of edifying. (Ephesians 4:29) The words that we speak are to build up, not tear down. Nothing corrupt is to come out of our mouths. Proverbs says the wise woman builds her house, but the foolish woman destroys hers with her own hands. (Proverbs 14:1) The words that we speak can either build or destroy. Some people suffer abuse within their homes that leaves no marks or bruises, but its wounds are just as severe. That is verbal abuse. Beating someone with words rather than fists leaves scars just the same, scars that can only be healed by the power of God. We must live our Christian lives 24 hours a day, 7 days a week, even at home. Women, use your words to bring healing and hope and help to those you love, instead of belittling them and wounding them and taking out the stresses and pressures of life on them. You are filled with the Spirit of God. You are a child of God. They should see how you live and glorify God, rather than wonder which one of you is real – the one in church or the one they see at home. There is no excuse! God has given you His own Holy Spirit. You can do all things through Christ who strengthens you.

Pressures of life are real, and they are felt most keenly perhaps at home. But do you suddenly empty yourself of the Holy Spirit when you walk through the door of your house? No! You are a child of God, a woman of God at home. And your spouse and your children should see your life of faith lived in its reality as they see you respond in the Spirit of God with the Word of God to the difficulties that come into every life. How is it that when someone calls you with a need, you can pray so earnestly for your prayer partner, and believe with them for their problem to be fixed, but when you have a problem you take it out on the whole family? Don't live your life so sweetly to impress others when your family suffers from your displays of rage or depression or discouragement. It means nothing for others to marvel at what a wonderful Christian you are when your own family just wonders what a

Christian is supposed to be. You can speak the Word to your problems at home. You should be controlled by the Holy Spirit, led by the Holy Spirit at home as well as at church. You have the power of God available to you wherever you are.

We must realize the power of the words that we speak over our children. We have seven children, no twins in the bunch, and I know the rigors of family life and schedules and terrific two's and wonderful teens – and being in the ministry! Sometimes you feel like you meet yourself coming and going! But in the midst of this busy life, we must continually watch what we say over our children. The Word works in dealing with family life, too! When one of our daughters was young, she was rather clumsy at times and it seemed like we couldn't get through a meal without a spill of some kind – usually milk! Now she was beyond the age of a sippy cup! So we had to just handle it! We reassured her it was OK, just try to be careful, as we wiped up the spill. We didn't label her a "milk-spiller", we didn't get upset about the mess, we just handled it calmly and pretty soon there were no more spills. When there were conflicts or disagreements between the children we handled them according to the Word. We made them repent and forgive one another. When they came to us with an "I want" we taught them to pray with us for their needs to be met. I remember once they wanted a little wading pool to play in one summer. We prayed with them and believed God that He would bring them a wading pool. Now at this particular time we had absolutely no extra money for anything. Our hearts were aching as parents, wishing we had the ability to simply go to the store and get one. But we believed God with them, and the next Sunday when we got home from church, guess what was sitting on the deck in the back of the house, a new little pool! That taught all of us a valuable lesson! God will meet our needs! When they had a little bump or bruise, we put a band-aid on, wiped away their tears and prayed with them that "by His stripes we are healed." This is how they learn to walk in faith in their own lives, by our training and example. Deuteronomy 6 says that we are to be teaching the commands to our children when we lie down and when we rise up – continually throughout each day we are to show them what it is to walk with God and to live by faith.

We spoke the Word of God over them from the womb. We called them men and women of God, treasures, gifts from God – not rugrats, nuisances, interruptions. When other Christians, even ministers, would question us regarding the size of our family ("You're pregnant again?") we reminded them the Word says that children are a heritage of the Lord, the fruit of the womb is His reward. We were thrilled as we watched each of them grow into wonderful men and women of God, working with us in the ministry and growing in the unique gifts that God placed in each of them. We continually encourage them to fulfill God's plan and design for their lives, bearing fruit for the Kingdom. They are workers in the ministry, tithers and givers, faithful to God. They have grown up knowing the power of the Word of God and faith that is lived daily. They have learned that this life of faith is real. God is a good God who has good things for His children.

As the children go through each stage of growth, we have raised them with the standard of the Word of God. When they were small, we taught them the Word and read Bible stories at bedtime. We disciplined them according to the Word. We taught them the difference between right and wrong. We taught them to respect authority – our authority as parents and the authority of the Word of God in all our lives. We trained them to be gentlemen and ladies, to be polite and considerate of others. During the teen years with urges for independence and wanting to be their own person, we walked with the Word of God as the standard, teaching them to seek God for their future and yield themselves to Him. During times of discussion about morality and current cultural trends, we have held them to the standard of God's Word. This takes the pressure off of us as parents. It's not just mom and dad being old fashioned and saying no to everything, it is the Word of God setting the standard for life and conduct. This gives them a pattern that they will follow the rest of their lives. When there is a question the answer is in the Word of God.

We began praying for the spouses of our children from their childhood. Two of our daughters are now married to wonderful men of God who are such loving, caring husbands – strong in faith and in the knowledge of God.

The Holy Spirit led them to one another, and confirmed in all our hearts that these were the spouses that He had prepared for them. As difficult as it is to place your daughter in the hands of a young man, these marriages were truly anointed as we felt the power of God confirming their union. And we feel so blessed to have these amazing men of God join our family. God is so good!

We still have children at home. We continue to live and speak the Word over them. Through the transitions of life, the Word of God is our constant source. We are watching it bear fruit in the lives of our precious children.

❧ CHAPTER 10 ❧
YOU HAVE AN ENEMY

"Be sober, be vigilant; because your adversary the devil, as a roaring lion, walketh about, seeking whom he may devour."

I Peter 5:8

You have an enemy. His name is Satan. He hates God and he hates you. As Peter says, he walks about like a roaring lion seeking whom he may devour. He wants to devour you, your family, your finances, your health, all that concerns you. Jesus said in John 10:10, "The thief cometh not, but for to steal, and to kill, and to destroy: I am come that they might have life, and that they might have it more abundantly." The devil, Satan, is the enemy of our souls. He doesn't want anyone to know God or follow Him. He certainly doesn't want you to enjoy the abundant life that Jesus came to give you. Part of walking by faith is learning that we have an enemy who is attacking us, who wants to take from us all that Jesus has given us as believers. We must understand that Jesus has already given us the victory over this enemy, and always leads us in triumph! (II Corinthians 2:14)

First, we must understand that Satan is a created being. He is not another god, only evil. He was created as an angel and lived in heaven with God. His name was Lucifer. (Isaiah 14:12) The Bible describes him in Ezekiel as the covering cherub who was on the holy mountain of God. He was beautiful, arrayed with all manner of jewels in settings of gold. (Ezekiel 28:13-14) He was lifted up with pride and wanted to be like God. As a result he was cast out of heaven, along with a third of the angels (Revelation 12:9). They were cast out of heaven because sin was found in them, and there is no sin in heaven. These fallen angels are what we call demons. Now it is very important that you understand these facts about Satan. He is not on an equal plane with God. He was created by God, an angelic being who lost his place in heaven because sin was found in him. The devil is not equal in power and ability with God – only evil. He was created by God. Just as we know that angels are not God, they are His servants, the devil is a fallen angel, limited in power and ability. For example, God is omniscient, He knows everything. He knows the past and the future. He knows all about you. The devil only knows what he sees and hears. God is omnipresent – everywhere at once. The devil can only be in one place at one time. God is omnipotent – all powerful. The devil's power is limited. And he has been completely defeated by the cross of Christ! Hallelujah!

As we said earlier, the devil hates you and wants to see you lose. He wanted his own following in heaven, and a third of the angels fell along with him. Now he is trying to get men to follow him as well. He hates God and he hates the crown of God's creation – man. He works through trickery and deceit to take souls captive. He does not want you to follow God, and if you do, he wants to keep you in discouragement and defeat. Many Christians, not knowing the truth of God's Word, attribute the devil's tactics to God. For example, when they get sick they say that God is trying to teach them something. They have to learn how to suffer, etc. These are lies from the devil himself. Jesus said there is none good but God. God is a good God. He does not make us sick. James says that God cannot be tempted with evil, neither does He tempt any man. (James 1:13) In the subsequent verses, James says that every good and perfect gift comes from God. God does not use the evil things of this world to correct us or teach us or try us. He corrects and instructs us through His Word. He does not use sickness, lack, loneliness or anything like that to accomplish His work in us. His work in us is done through His Word and by His Spirit.

Let's look at the beginning. God created the earth and when He was finished He declared that it was very good. God made all that we see, and all of it was good. He made Adam and Eve and placed them in the beautiful Garden of Eden where all they had to do was rule and reign, have dominion, and enjoy sweet fellowship daily with God. They were the King and Queen of earth and all that God had made was theirs to enjoy. They didn't have to work or labor for their provision, God gave them all they needed in abundance. Then the devil, who had been kicked out of heaven, appeared on the scene. He appeared as a beautiful serpent and through temptation he persuaded Adam and Eve to disobey God. As a result, sin entered the world for the first time. This beautiful, perfect Eden that God had created for the enjoyment and supply of the King and Queen of earth was now marred by sin. Now they would die, instead of living forever with God. And all creation became subject to death. The devil obtained an entrance into this earth through

Adam's disobedience. However, God has always known that He would ultimately rule and reign forever. Even in the Garden of Eden as God was pronouncing sentence on Adam and Eve and the enemy, He declared that in the end He would win again. He made the serpent to crawl on his belly and eat dust. He said that there would be continual enmity between the serpent and the woman. He said that her Seed would bruise the head of the serpent! (Genesis 3:14-15) Glory to God! From the very beginning, the devil knew that he was doomed. He knew that there would come a Man, born of a woman, who would crush him.

That Man was Jesus, the Son of God. He came in the flesh to redeem us, to purchase us again for God. His blood paid the price for our sins so that the devil has nothing against us. God Himself has declared us righteous by the blood of Jesus. Romans 5:19 describes the transaction, by the disobedience of one (Adam) sin entered the world. Through the obedience of One (Jesus) are many declared righteous. We are now once again the sons and daughters of God. As Adam and Eve were created in the Garden in perfection, we are made perfect by the blood of Jesus. When Jesus came into the world, He lived a perfect life. In that perfection, He took upon Himself the sin of all mankind so that through Him we have redemption, justification, a life with God. When I was growing up and going through catechism class at church, the dear minister who taught me the meaning of justification said, "It is just as if I never sinned." Jesus became sin for us, so that we might be made the righteousness of God in Him.

It was through His death that the enemy, Satan, has been defeated. The Bible says that in the cross, Jesus defeated all the power of the enemy. Colossians 2:13-15 declares to us,

"And you, being dead in your sins and the uncircumcision of your flesh, hath he quickened together with Him, having forgiven you all trespasses; blotting out the handwriting of ordinances that was against us, which was contrary to us, and took it out of the way, nailing it to His cross; and having spoiled principalities and powers, He made a show of them openly, triumphing over them in it." Glory Hallelujah! Jesus defeated the enemy, spoiled principalities and powers in the cross. In Paul's letter to the Ephesians, he describes his prayer for the Ephesian church, that their eyes would be opened to the wonderful truths of the gospel. "And what is the exceeding greatness of His power to us-ward who believe, according to the working of His mighty power, which He wrought in Christ, when He raised Him from the dead, and set Him at His own right hand in the heavenly places, far above all principality, and power, and might, and dominion, and every name that is named, not only in this world, but also in that which is to come: and hath put all things under His feet, and gave Him to be the head over all things to the church, which is His body, the fulness of Him that filleth all in all." (Ephesians 1:19-23) Let your heart rejoice in this revelation. Through the death, burial and resurrection of Jesus, we have victory over the enemy. Jesus is seated at the right hand of God "far above all principality, and power, and might, and dominion. . ." In other words, there is no power above Jesus. There is no might above Jesus' might. There is no dominion over Jesus. Through His death and resurrection He has defeated the enemy and has been seated in the victor's seat far above any power on earth. There is nothing that the devil can do to Jesus. Jesus has won the victory.

The book of Revelation gives us a clear picture through the

words of Jesus Himself as He is speaking to John. Jesus said, "I am He that liveth, and was dead; and, behold, I am alive for evermore. Amen; and have the keys of hell and of death." Jesus has the keys of hell and of death. He completely defeated the enemy and now holds the keys to the enemy's domain. Jesus died and was buried. During the time that His body was in the tomb, He went into hell and defeated the devil. Then Jesus was raised again as proof of that victory and the completion of His triumph over all the power of the enemy. Then he took the holy blood that He had shed and poured it on the altar in heaven to remain forever the sacrifice for sin for all mankind. Hebrews 9:11-12 says, "But Christ being come an high priest of good things to come, by a greater and more perfect tabernacle, not made with hands, that is to say, not of this building; neither by the blood of goats and calves, but by His own blood He entered in once into the holy place, having obtained eternal redemption for us." Chapter 10 verse 12 goes on to say, "But this Man, after He had offered one sacrifice for sins forever, sat down on the right hand of God;" Again God has written in His Word that Jesus is seated at the right hand of God. He has completed the work He was given to do, and now He is seated at God's own right hand far above any power that is on this earth. Jesus was given the place of authority, at the right hand of God, because He secured it for Himself with His victory on the cross and His resurrection from the dead. Not only that, but He took the holy blood that He shed and poured it on the heavenly altar as a sacrifice for sin for all mankind forever!

What does this mean for us today? Look at Colossians 1:12-14, "Giving thanks unto the Father, which hath made us meet to be partakers of the inheritance of the saints in light: Who hath delivered us from the power of darkness and hath translated us into the kingdom of His dear Son: in Whom we have redemption through His blood, even the forgiveness of sins:" Glory to God! He has delivered us out of the power of darkness and vaulted us into His own kingdom! We are delivered from the power of the enemy. We have redemption through the holy blood of Jesus, which made the way for us. In that cross, Jesus triumphed over all the power of the enemy, and openly displayed His victory for all to see. Through that victory, we have been delivered from the power of the enemy, transferred into the kingdom of God. The devil has no legal ground in me. By virtue of the sacrifice of Jesus, I have been declared not guilty and have been taken out of the very realm of power of darkness. Not only that, but Ephesians 2:4-7 says, "But God, who is rich in mercy, for His great love wherewith He loved us, even when we were dead in sins, hath quickened us together with Christ, (by grace ye are saved;) and hath raised us up together, and made us sit together in heavenly places in Christ Jesus: that in the ages to come He might show the exceeding riches of His grace in His kindness toward us through Christ Jesus." Hallelujah! Not only are we saved, but we are raised up together, and seated in heavenly places in Christ Jesus! Jesus is seated in the place of authority at God's right hand, and we are seated with Him in heavenly places! We share completely in His victory, not just when we die, but the moment we are born again this is our position. We are seated in heavenly places in Christ Jesus. Physically, we are still on this earth, but in the spirit we share in the victory that Jesus wrought when He died and rose again. We are seated with Christ in that place of authority. So we have all authority over the enemy. We have authority over sickness and disease and temptation and lack and discouragement and depression, over any tactic that the devil would try to use to defeat us. Understand the truth of these scriptures. The devil has no authority over you. Jesus has already placed you in a position of power over all the power of the enemy. When you received Jesus as your Savior, when you became a child of God, you became a part of His kingdom which places you in a position of authority over all the power of the enemy. Remember, you are seated with Him in heavenly places – far above all principality and power and might and dominion. This is part of your inheritance, your identity as a child of God and a citizen in His Kingdom.

In this life we face opposition from many sides. There are difficulties to be faced. But the Bible tells us that we do not wrestle with flesh and blood. In other words, our opposition isn't from people, but from the forces of the enemy working through people to try to discourage us and defeat us in our walk with Christ. We are in a war, a battle the outcome of which is already determined. The devil has already been defeated and ultimately will forever burn in the lake of fire. But while we are here on this earth he is roaming about like a roaring lion, seeking whom he may devour. He wants to devour your life, your joy, your provision; anything to hurt you and get you to turn away from God.

But the Scripture goes on to say that the weapons of this warfare are not carnal, that is they are not physical weapons with which we face our foe, but they are mighty through God to the pulling down of strongholds, bringing into captivity every thought to the obedience of Christ. (II Corinthians 10:4-5) We do not arm ourselves with weapons of destruction on a physical level, but our weapons are spiritual and mighty through God. Our weapons can pull down strongholds, places where the enemy has entrenched himself. We do not fight this battle in our own strength. Our weapons are mighty through God! Hallelujah!

Ephesians 6:10-18 gives us a look at the arsenal of weapons available to us.

- The belt of truth – to strengthen our backs to stand in battle

- The breastplate of righteousness – to shield our hearts from hurts and wounds. No matter what others may say about us, we know that we stand as the righteousness of God.

- The combat boots of the Gospel – we are ready to go to preach the Good News.

- The shield of faith – we have a force-field of faith which quenches all the fiery missiles of the evil one.

- The helmet of salvation – protects our minds and our thought-life. We think about those things that are good and wholesome. We are able to cast down imaginations and every high thing that exalts itself against the knowledge of God. (II Corinthians 10:5)

- The sword of the Spirit – the Word of God. When we speak the Word in the midst of life situations, the enemy feels the blade! We bring the power of God on the scene to change circumstances and maintain victory. Notice, this is our only offensive weapon. We use the Word of God and stand in our authority to bring the power of God to rout the enemy. We repel his attacks, and then use the Word to drive Him out and away from our circumstances.

What does all this mean to us today? It means that we are not defenseless against the attack of the enemy. We have been given spiritual weapons for this spiritual battle. Paul was describing the armor of a Roman soldier of the day, completely outfitted from head to toe. Picture yourself as a combat soldier of the present, covered with armor with the latest technological advances. God has given us all that we need to fight this fight of faith and win the battle against the spiritual forces that come against us. Ephesians 6:11 says, "Put on the whole armor of God, that ye may be able to stand against the wiles of the devil." We are given this armor so we can win! We can stand against the tricks and deceits of the enemy. We don't have to live in defeat, discouragement, depression or fear. God has given us this heavenly armor so that we can successfully stand against anything the enemy tries to use against us.

Now I don't want to overemphasize this part of the Christian life. There are some who are always chasing devils instead of enjoying their life with God. They are always in combat maneuvers fighting every step of the way, rather than walking in the abundant life Jesus has provided. Let me reiterate, Jesus has already defeated the enemy. While we are on this earth we will be attacked, but Jesus has already given us the victory! We must know who we are in Christ, and know the power and authority that we walk in as His children to successfully stand up against the tricks of the enemy. Many Christians have given up the fight when in truth they are more than conquerors through him that loved us. (Romans 8:37) As we said at the beginning of the chapter, the enemy walks about like a roaring lion seeking whom he may devour. We must be aware of his devices. He wants to devour us, steal from us, do us harm. But we have the victory! No matter what he tries against us, Jesus has already defeated him and rendered him powerless in our lives. We must simply stand in the authority given us as children of God, with the Name and the Word and the blood of Jesus. I take my cue from the life of Christ as recorded in the gospels. Jesus didn't go around looking for the enemy. The devil came against Him in many different ways. From the time of temptation in the wilderness, throughout Jesus' earthly ministry, until the final defeat of the enemy at the cross, the devil tried to trap Jesus and destroy Him. The Bible records that from early in His public ministry, the religious people around Jesus plotted together how they could destroy Him. (Matthew 12:14) On every occasion, Jesus simply handled the situation, quoting the Word, commanding demons to leave, healing the sick, raising the dead. In the same way, I don't go around looking for demons, but when the enemy comes against me in any form, I stand in the authority given me as a child of God to drive off his attack. "Ye are of God, little children, and have overcome them: because greater is He that is in you than he that is in the world." (I John 4:4) Notice this verse says that we have overcome them. The defeat of the devil has been accomplished. We have overcome them. Why? Because the Greater One, Jesus, lives on the inside of us! The One who defeated the enemy on his own territory lives on the inside of us by His Spirit. We can walk in complete victory everyday!

❧ CHAPTER 11 ❧
THE TIMING OF THE LORD

"But, beloved, do not forget this one thing, that with the Lord one day is as a thousand years, and a thousand years as one day. The Lord is not slack concerning His promise, as some count slackness, but is longsuffering toward us, not willing that any should perish but that all should come to repentance."

II Peter 3:8-9

One of the hardest things about walking this walk of faith is the time factor. We pray and believe and guard our hearts and watch our words, and we wait for the Lord to act. The waiting time between believing and seeing is the longest time on earth! It is during this time that the devil sows seeds of doubt regarding the promises of God and your faith to believe Him. During this time we are tempted to give up on God and figure out some other way to do it ourselves. If it doesn't happen in the timeframe we have set, we are tempted to stop believing altogether. So it is important that we look at the Word regarding the timing of the Lord.

In His Revelation to John, chapter one verse eight, Jesus declares, "I am the Alpha and the Omega, the Beginning and the End, who is and who was and who is to come, the Almighty." God encompasses all of time. He is the Beginning and the End. He created the world and He knows the day when it will end. He has all of time before Him. There are no surprises with God. There are no unexpected events. God already knows what will happen and has prepared for it.

Isaiah 46:9-10 says, "Remember the former things of old, For I am God, and there is no other; I am God, and there is none like Me, declaring the end from the beginning, and from ancient times things that are not yet done, saying, 'My counsel shall stand, and I will do all My pleasure.'" God declares the end from the beginning. He already knows what will come to pass. So our lifetime is within that span – from beginning to end. When we pray, it is within that timeframe – beginning to end. So we can trust that God, who already knows tomorrow and has declared the end from the beginning, will work within the time that is needed to bring to pass His perfect will. When we pray, we can know that God has heard our prayer and is acting according to His perfect plan for us and for all concerned.

II Peter 3:8-9 gives us a glimpse of God's concept of time. It says that with God one day is as a thousand years and a thousand years are as one day. In other words, God sees all of history before Him at once. Looking forward years or centuries are like looking for tomorrow. Now He knows we don't have a thousand years to wait! But in this Scripture we see that God sees the big picture. He sees all of time. And the answer to our prayer fits into that big picture. The Scripture continues to say that God is not slack concerning

His promises, but He is longsuffering. In other words, God is patient. He is not slacking on His Word, but He is patiently waiting for the right time. His primary goal is for all to come to repentance, to know Him.

Isaiah 55:8-11 reveals to us that God's ways are not our ways, and His thoughts are not our thoughts. They are higher! Hallelujah! He is God! In our society of instant everything we must remember that His ways are not our ways. He is working in His way, according to the complete plan He has already declared. Then the Lord shows us the effectiveness of His Word. Just as rain and snow fall to the ground to water the earth and make it fruitful, His Word that has been spoken will be fruitful in our lives to bring to pass His will and the answer to our prayers. The Word will not bounce back, it will not return to Him empty, it will produce fruit! Amen! So as we pray and wait, we know that the Word is working to bring results in our lives. Don't let the devil convince you that it's not working, it's no use. Remember, the Word is working, even as you are waiting for the results. He says that His Word will accomplish its purpose. It will be successful in that thing for which it was sent. While you are waiting the Word will work. We have God's promise on it! He declares that His Word produces fruit, just as rain makes the earth bring forth a harvest that gives seed to the sower and bread for food. Notice that God uses the example of seed and fruit. Anyone who has planted a seed knows that it takes time to bring that seed to germination and growth and budding and fruit-bearing. It takes time! So don't give up during the waiting period. God is working to bring His Word to pass. We also know by experience that if you dig up a seed every other day or so to see how it is doing, constantly wondering if it has sprouted yet, you will eventually kill the seed. So it is with our prayers. Don't keep going back to God, asking if He is sure this is all going to work. You must stand and believe and wait upon Him! He is working in ways you cannot see to bring the result, the desired end.

While we are talking about seeds and fruit, it is important to remember that there are natural times and seasons and cycles that God has already set in place in the creation of the earth. Genesis 8:22 says, "While the earth remains, seedtime and harvest, cold and heat, winter and summer, and day and night shall not cease." God has given us day and night and the seasons of the year. These are times and cycles that are already established in the earth. Ecclesiastes 3:1-8 tells us that there is a season for everything and a time for every purpose under heaven: a time to be born, and a time to die; a time to plant, and a time to pluck what is planted; etc. God created the earth and its cycles. There are normal seasons which He has established. There is a time for everything. There is a time for your prayer to be answered, for your desire to be fulfilled. We must wait for the right time!

God works according to the natural cycles He has set in place. In Genesis 18:10 and 14, God says, "I will certainly return to you according to the time of life, and behold, Sarah your wife shall have a son." He repeats in verse 14, "Is anything too hard for the Lord? At the appointed time I will return to you, according to the time of life, and Sarah shall have a son." Now notice that God promised a child to this elderly couple who had been barren all these years. He worked a miracle in their bodies. But He also worked "according to the time of life." In other words, we know it takes time for conception, and nine months for that life to be carried in the womb. There is a time of life. God has set the cycles and seasons in place. He worked a miracle for Abraham and Sarah, and He did it according to the time of life. God can work within natural seasons to bring to pass the desire of our hearts.

Daniel 2:20-23 says that God changes the times and the seasons. This is according to God's plan, God's doing. He removes kings and raises up kings. God has everything under control! Verse 22 says, "He reveals deep and secret things; He knows what is in the darkness, and light dwells with Him." There is nothing hidden from God. While we are waiting, we can be sure that nothing gets past Him. There is nothing that the enemy can sneak by Him. God is taking care of every detail, and revealing the deep and secret things to us as we wait upon Him. You know, with that revelation comes a responsibility to trust God to bring it to pass. We want the gifts of the Spirit and the revelation of the things of God, and we must use our faith accordingly. When we receive revelation of things to come, we must wait upon God to see those things fulfilled, and not complain while we are waiting. What an honor to have the gifts of the Spirit given to us, and revelation of the plans and purposes of God! It is a small thing to simply wait upon God and believe that He will bring to pass what He has revealed!

As we have seen in the Word of God, God has all of time before Him. He declares the end from the beginning. God sees the big picture. And we must remember that we are only a part of that picture. There are other people and factors involved in the answers to our prayers. Remember the Shunammite woman we read about earlier? Well, she was instructed by the prophet Elisha, the same man who had raised her son from the dead, to move away from her home to another place for the duration of a seven-year famine. At the end of seven years she returned to reclaim her home and lands. As she went to appeal to the king for the return of her property, Gehazi, the servant of Elisha, was reciting to the king the story of her son who was raised from the dead. Just as he was finishing the story, in walks the Shunammite woman! Gehazi said, "My lord, O king, this is the woman, and this is her son whom Elisha restored to life." Talk about timing! Of course, the king ordered that her lands be restored to her, along with the profit of the harvest of seven years while she had been gone. Consider all the pieces that had to fall into place for this event to occur. The woman had to return at precisely that time. The king had to ask, and Gehazi had to tell that story at precisely that moment! Take courage! While you are waiting, God is bringing all the pieces of the puzzle together in the precise fashion and the perfect time for your prayer to be answered! God is arranging things in perfect order. Be patient. He does all things well!

God works within normal circumstances, but he can work outside of them as well. Nothing is impossible with God! In the book of Joshua, we read of a particular battle with the Amorites. God was already at work, helping Joshua to win the battle by throwing hailstones from heaven on the Amorite army! The Israelites were finishing the battle, when Joshua commanded the sun and moon to stand still so they could complete the job. So the sun stood still for a day, while the Israelites completed their mission. Now we know from modern physics that the sun doesn't move, the earth moves. We know that it is the earth's rotation which gives us day and night and also the force of gravity. If the earth stopped, all physical forces would be gone, and there would be nothing to hold us here. So, God had to hold this planet and everything on it during that day that Joshua fought the battle. Glory! That same God is working on your behalf to answer your prayers and to bring His Word to pass in your life!

A similar event occurred in the ministry of Isaiah. He had warned King Hezekiah of his impending death, and the king appealed to God for longer life. God heard his prayer, and sent Isaiah back to tell him that God would give him fifteen more years. As a sign to Hezekiah that his life would indeed be lengthened, God said He would literally turn back time by ten degrees on the sundial. Again, we see that God is in command of the forces of nature. He can work with them or He can command them to turn back! How great is our God!

Isaiah 60:22 says, "A little one shall become a thousand, and a small one a strong nation. I, the Lord, will hasten it in its time." God can speed the clock as well as turn it back! In the course of time, God can make sure that events will happen with precision – and He has all power to make His Word come to pass. Even though the situation may look impossible, the Lord is able to fulfill His promise. In II Kings 7, the Lord reversed a famine that was so severe they were paying to eat a donkey's head or dove's droppings. In the first verse, the Lord promised that the situation would be completely changed "tomorrow." Instead of eating refuse, they would have fine flour and grain. Imagine that, today you are eating dove's droppings and God promises that tomorrow you will have plenty of fine flour and grain. God can change your situation overnight! As we read the rest of the chapter, we see that God indeed fulfilled His Word and they had plenty!

Now what does this all mean for you? First of all, we can be assured that God has a perfect plan. Esther 4:14 says,

"... Yet who knows whether you have come to the kingdom for such a time as this?" You have a purpose and it is for this time and this hour. God has made His design from the beginning, and has already declared it. Your place in His plan is assured. Psalm 139:16 says, "Your eyes saw my substance, being yet unformed. And in Your book they all were written, the days fashioned for me, when as yet there were none of them." God has fashioned your days for you before you lived one of them. You can trust that His timing is perfect. Although to you it may seem that you are waiting a long time, God has fashioned each day for you and knows the right time for each event.

Then, it is imperative that you obey God. Obey His voice. This takes faith! Remember the Israelites as they journeyed from Egypt to the Promised Land. God had given them a great deliverance from slavery. He promised to lead them to their own land, a land of abundance, a land flowing with milk and honey. All they had to do was to go into the land and possess it. But what happened when they reached the border of the land? They refused to go in. They believed the circumstances rather than the promises of God. Because they disobeyed God, He turned them around and told them they would spend 40 years wandering in the desert, until all of the unbelievers perished. When you disobey God, you may cause delays in His plan for you. Like when you miss your turn on the highway, you have to backtrack. Or you try to get there another way and end up driving around and taking twice as long as you would have. You must obey God and act on His Word quickly.

Thirdly, you must have endurance. In Matthew 24, Jesus says, "But he who endures to the end shall be saved." There is an end! But you must endure to the end. You must endure to see the result of your faith. Don't give up! God has the perfect plan for you. He has already set it in motion. He has declared the end from the beginning. Don't give up in the middle! Wait until you reach the goal! Your faith will be rewarded. Proverbs 13:12 says, "Hope deferred makes the heart sick, but when the desire comes, it is a tree of life." It's not easy to wait. Hope deferred, hope delayed makes the heart sick. But when the desire comes – when the desire comes – it is a tree of life. When you see the end of your faith, it will bless you and minister to you and encourage you and build you in such a wonderful way. Celebrate the fulfillment! Celebrate the victory!

God sees and declares the end from the beginning. We only see one moment at a time, one day at a time. This is a great part of our walk of faith, to trust Him through each day, believing that despite circumstances to the contrary His plan will be accomplished. Ps. 102:12-13 says, "But thou, O Lord, shalt endure for ever; and thy remembrance unto all generations. Thou shalt arise and have mercy upon Zion: for the time to favor her, yea, the set time, is come." God is everlasting, eternal, forever. He remembers all generations from Adam and Eve until now and beyond. And within that span of memory He has a set time for you. The time to favor you, the set time, is come! He has set times in your life when those dreams will become reality. Because you are His child, you believe in Him, you trust Him; you can know that those times for fulfillment are set and established in His plan. God will fulfill what He has promised you.

God has placed eternity in our hearts. We are His children. We will live forever with Him. But in this earth we are creatures of time. We are to be aware of the limitations of time. There are only so many days we have to live. Ephesians 5:16 in the Amplified Bible says, "Making the most of the time [buying up each opportunity], because the days are evil." We must use the time that we have on this earth to live a life that brings glory to God. As we seek Him, as we follow Him, we will use each moment to fulfill His will for our lives. That is making the most of the time.

Habakuk 2:2-4 is a tremendous help in understanding the timing of the Lord. These verses assure us that the vision is yet for an appointed time, though it tarry wait for it. It will come, it will not delay. When God has given you a vision, when you are standing on His Word, you can write it down and make record of it. Though it tarries – although it takes longer than you expected, God says wait for it! You can be sure that you won't be disappointed. God will not let you down. It will come. It will not delay. Now it may seem delayed to you, but God says to wait. It will come! God is faithful. He has spoken it, and He will do it!

The Bible says that we need to be followers of those who through faith and patience inherit the promises. We come into our inheritance, the fulfillment of God's promises, through faith and patience. God has only the best for us, and it is worth waiting for! The Bible says that as we are waiting on the Lord, we can renew our strength, mounting up with wings as eagles. We shall run and not be weary. We shall walk and not faint. (Isaiah 40:31) We can walk all the way to the end, right into the fulfillment of our hopes and dreams. We have the Lord's strength to renew us day by day. Don't give up! The timing of the Lord is perfect, and He will complete that which He has begun in you! (Philippians 1:6)

๛ CHAPTER 12 ๏
SILLY WOMEN

*"For of this sort are they which creep into houses, and
lead captive silly women laden with sins, led away
with divers lusts, ever learning, and never able to come
to the knowledge of the truth."*

II Timothy 3:6-7

The Word of God is so good! God gives us warning of the
pitfalls all around us so that we can walk successfully in this
life. Now this Scripture is one that may seem to be hard on
the surface, calling us "silly women", but we need to read and
heed! Notice in the first verses of II Timothy 3 that Paul
is warning against the people of this day who are "lovers of
pleasures more than lovers of God" (vs. 4), men who have a
form of godliness but deny its power. (vs. 5) This is the
kind of person Paul is warning against, this one leads captive
silly women laden with sins. Now ladies, we need to be
aware of the devices of the enemy. As we have learned, we
have an enemy who is roaming about seeking whom he may
devour. He wants to take us captive and keep us in bondage.

These verses warn us that as women, we need to be aware of people like this and examine ourselves. Notice, these silly women are laden with sins, led away with divers lusts. Sin is a problem we must deal with. We cannot ignore sin in our lives, we must face it and deal with it according to the Word. We live in an environment of permissibility. Lifestyles that were considered sinful just a few years ago are now "alternative." As pastors, we have met with couples who have lived together before being married and think that's ok. It's not called sin anymore, or fornication, it's just part of the process of dating and getting to know each other. They even have children together and feel no embarrassment. We must stand on the Word of God in every area, including the difficult ones. Sin is still sin. Adultery, fornication, gossip, lying, cheating, stealing, these are still wrong. These are sins that will hold you back and keep you from the Kingdom of God. When we do not deal with sin in our lives, we leave a door wide open to the enemy. He walks right in and takes us captive. He bewitches us with the current cultural trends and friends who say it's ok, and then we are caught in his trap. He takes full advantage of us and puts us in bondage. Notice this verse says that there are people who take advantage of silly women who are "laden with sins." Evidently, this type of woman doesn't recognize sin or want to deal with it effectively. She is laden down with sin. She is burdened with sin. As believers we know that Jesus bore our sins on the cross. How do we deal with sin? I John 1:9 says, "If we confess our sins, he is faithful and just to forgive us our sins and to cleanse us from all unrighteousness." When we sin we are to deal with it immediately by confessing it to God and allow Him to cleanse us with the precious blood of His Son. The Bible warns us against trying to hide our sin. We cannot hide from God. He knows what is going on in our lives. He has provided the answer for us, but we must yield to the Holy Spirit and repent quickly. Don't allow the enemy to obtain a foothold. We are not to give place to the devil. Consciously ignoring sin, trying to go on as though it didn't matter, is living a lie. We ourselves open the door to the enemy to kill, steal and destroy (John 10:10).

Notice these women are not only laden down with sin but they are led away with divers lusts. When you give place to the enemy by ignoring sin, you are easily led away with fleshly desires. The enemy is right there to keep you away from God and to lead you down a path of destruction. You are no longer walking by the Spirit, you are being led by the flesh and its lusts. This is a dangerous path. There are some who never recover. They continually walk farther away from God. Please heed the warning of the Scripture. James 1:14-15 tells us, "But everyman is tempted, when he is drawn away of his own lust, and enticed. Then when lust hath conceived, it bringeth forth sin: and sin, when it is finished, bringeth forth death." Do not be like these who are led away by lust down a path that ultimately ends in death. Jesus has provided the way for us to walk in righteousness. He has redeemed us by His own blood. We must walk in a manner that is pleasing to Him.

Notice these silly women are always learning, but never able to come to the knowledge of the truth. In previous chapters we have discussed the importance of receiving the Word and acting upon it, yet there seem to be people who are continually looking for something new, something else. They are ever learning but they are never able to come to the knowledge of the truth. The Word is the truth! We need to make the decision in our hearts to believe the Word of God and to receive it as the final authority in our lives. In these days you can find all kinds of teaching. Jesus warned us that the last days, the days before His coming, would be full of deceptive doctrine. (Matthew 24) Paul said that in the last days people would heap to themselves teachers, having itching ears. (II Timothy 4:3) That's right, heap up. There are so many ministers teaching so much stuff that you can heap them up. You can pick any kind of doctrine you want. People want to hear what they like to hear, what pleases them, what sounds good. So they will keep looking, surfing channels, reading books, going to conferences, until they find someone they like. They don't consider whether teaching lines up with the Word of God, they just want to hear what they like to hear. To be a woman of faith, you must walk by the Word of God – period. God says it – that settles it! You can hear all kinds of teaching from all kinds of doctrine, but the Word of God will never fail you. The Word of God is the only truth. The first question you must ask when you are listening to a teaching is – does this line up with the Word? It doesn't matter if the minister is eloquent and impressive, what is he saying? Many times messages will be emotionally charged, but only serve to keep you in the realm of self-pity. All of us have had hurt in our lives. Don't just sit and nurse your hurt and try to examine and psychoanalyze your hurt and evaluate the extent of your hurt – walk by the Word! Forgive! Release those who have hurt you! Get up and go on with God! Don't sit in the cesspool of the past a moment longer. Let the Spirit of the Lord minister to you, to heal you where you hurt. Let Jesus pour in the oil and the wine. Remember, the moment you say yes to Jesus, you are a new creature, a new creation altogether. As you allow the Holy Spirit to bring that revelation to you, you will see that the past can no longer hold you. You are free to live life as never before. He whom the Son sets free is free indeed! (John 8:36)

Many times the urge is to be in on the latest teaching or the latest move. God is moving everywhere! Stay where God has put you. Be faithful to the local work. God will show Himself to you right where you are! Now don't misunderstand, I am not saying that you should never go to conferences or go to hear other ministers. There are great men and women of God who have wonderful ministries who can impart to you from the Spirit of God. You need to make the effort to hear what God is saying through His ministers in these last days. I am warning that you watch your heart, and realize that God wants you to receive from Him and from the minister that He has placed over you primarily. You don't need to race here and there looking for the latest word, or the newest revelation. Receive from God on a daily basis right where you are. Don't be a silly woman, running hither and yon, unstable in life and a source of confusion to those around her. God knows your address! He knows where you live! He longs to reveal Himself to you right where you are! Walk on the solid rock of God's Word, consistent and faithful. Your life will bear fruit that is pleasing to God and will be a great testimony to all who are watching you.

Sometimes there is the temptation to think that the Word hasn't worked yet, or this promise hasn't been fulfilled yet, so there might be something new over here or over there that will cause God to work in your life. Many times I have heard Christians say, "If I can just have this person pray for me, then I will be healed, then my answer will come." God does give gifts to us, men of God with His anointing, to minister to us, but He can also heal you right where you are. God is faithful! He will perform His Word for you! Stand strong and see the salvation of the Lord! He will bring it to pass! He loves you. He knows your heart. He sees your tears. He hears and answers prayer. God is for you! And if God be for us, who can be against us!

Don't be a silly woman that everyone talks about. Don't be another example of instability. Make the decision to stand upon the Word and allow the love of God to uphold you and shine through you. He is faithful. You can rest upon His promises. You can stand in faith and see the power of God at work in your life.

❦ CHAPTER 13 ❧
PROVERBS 31 WOMAN

Of course, no book on women of faith would be complete without examining Proverbs 31, and there are entire books written on just this woman! But I would like to look at a few principles that are shared in the example of this woman given in Proverbs 31.

First of all, she is virtuous. The Hebrew word for virtuous is "hayil," strong in all moral qualities. As women of faith, we are strong women in every area, especially strong morally. We should know what is right according to the Word of God and run our households accordingly, setting the standard for our families. Don't be afraid to say "No!" even when "everybody else is doing it." There is much said about "family values" these days, and we are responsible to help teach and keep those values. As we discussed previously in this book, regardless of your upbringing or your past, you are a new creature. You <u>can</u> live right. You can teach your children to live right. Don't let past mistakes determine your future. Many of us grew up in the wild 60's and 70's with "free love" and "if it feels good, do it." We may have made mistakes, but don't allow that past to prevent you from taking a strong stand for morality now. You are a virtuous woman because of the blood of Jesus! The Word of God is your standard for living. Be strong morally, strong enough to say no to wrong.

The virtuous woman brings a sense of peace and security to her husband – so that he will have no lack of gain. "The heart of her husband safely trusts in her, so that he shall have no lack of gain." (vs. 11) In the home, we know the order established by the Lord. The husband is the head of the home as Christ is the head of the church. A woman of faith will do all she can to minister to her husband, to show him that she is able to be trusted. When your husband can trust you, knowing that the house is taken care of, the children are all right, he can be free to focus on his work so that he will have no lack of gain. Marriage takes trust from both parties. We must do all we can to be sure that we can be trusted. Now I realize that it goes both ways. Many times there are husbands who hide things from their wives to the devastation of the relationship. But I am speaking to the women – do your part to be trustworthy. See to your responsibilities. Make an effort at being open to your husband and discreet with family matters. Many times the husband becomes the center of gossip around the coffee table, or over the phone. Don't tell others private things that would embarrass your husband or harm his reputation. Your husband must feel safe in sharing things with you, confident that you will keep them to yourself – or he may stop sharing.

She is an industrious woman, using the resources at hand to take care of her household. This is a primary responsibility with women. They are the caretakers and nest-keepers! We read in this passage of Proverbs a description of how a virtuous woman will take care of the needs of her family – gathering food, working with her hands, investing in real estate, planting seed, sewing beautiful clothing for herself and her household and more to sell. Verse 13 says that she works willingly with her hands. Women are workers! We have multiple responsibilities. This is a busy lady! Note that she is not just at home, but is involved in business efforts as well. In all these endeavors she is seeking the welfare of her household. "She is not afraid of the snow for her household: for all her household are clothed with scarlet." (Verse 21) She has prepared well for the expected changes in life, the changes of seasons, so she is not worried about what tomorrow will bring.

This woman has helped her husband to achieve a place of leadership in the community because of her support at home. Verse 23 says, "Her husband is known in the gates among the elders of the land." When you are a virtuous woman, your support at home helps your husband to succeed in life. He is an able, respected leader at home so he can be an able, respected leader in the community. His self-confidence is continually built up at home so that he can go out and be strong in the community. Without that support at home, or with negative pressure, it is much harder for a man to be successful. I have known women who have literally destroyed their husbands by continually berating them for lack of money or lack of time. The man is doing all he can to provide for his family and what does he hear at home? "Is this all there is? How are we going to pay the bills? Can't you make more money?" This woman is tearing down her husband with her words. If his own wife doesn't believe in him or support him, how do you expect him to be strong on his job and in the community? A virtuous woman gives support to her husband so that he has confidence to go to his job and be successful, and be a leader in the community.

The important attributes of this woman are not seen in her business accomplishments, but in her strength and honor and wisdom. She is clothed with strength and honor, and she speaks with wisdom. Her words are kind words. (Remember the chapter on the importance of the words we speak!) How wonderful – to hear a kind word or two in the midst of a difficult day! This woman of God is built up in her faith so that out of the abundance of her heart her mouth speaks. She speaks with wisdom and kindness because her heart is full of the love of God. She can minister words of encouragement no matter how difficult things may seem, because she puts her trust in the Lord. And in the end the most wonderful reward of all, her children rise up and bless her and her husband praises her. (Verse 28) Although you may live many thankless days, in the end your reward will be evident to all. Your children will thank you for raising them to fear the Lord. Your husband will honor you for what you have done to serve God and your family. "Charm is deceitful, and beauty is vain: but a woman that feareth the Lord, she shall be praised." (Verse 30) The bottom line of this woman's life is that she fears the Lord. With all the responsibilities and accomplishments described, the most important is that she fears the Lord. With that relationship with God as her foundation, her reward is secure. Her life is a life of faith free from worry and fear. And that will be obvious to all.

❧ CHAPTER 14 ❧
KEEPERS AT HOME

"That they admonish the young women to love their husbands, to love their children, to be discreet, chaste, homemakers, good, obedient to their own husbands, that the word of God may not be blasphemed."

Titus 2:4-5

In his instructions to Titus, a young pastor in the early church, Paul encourages the older women to teach the younger women how to properly manage themselves and their households. This passage describes some of our basic duties as women, that we love our husband and children, be discreet and chaste and be homemakers. We have reviewed the Proverbs 31 woman and her resourcefulness and I want to emphasize in this chapter the importance of homemaking. The King James version says that we are to be "keepers at home." I like those words. Women, we keep our homes. We keep them clean and safe and full of love and light and the glory of God. No matter what other responsibilities we accept into our lives, it is our assignment to keep our homes.

I realize that most families have both husband and wife working outside the home, juggling work schedules and other activities and many men share in the chores at home. This is wonderful! It is great to see a husband pitching in with dishes or laundry or making a meal. That is a real plus to the family life and the equalization of the pressures of daily responsibilities. But I want to emphasize the importance of the woman's role in keeping the home. As women of faith we choose to walk according to the Word of God, and this is the Word regarding home life. Women are to be homemakers. That does not exclude you from having a career or outside activities, but it does admonish us that the home is our responsibility. Over the years, the opportunities available to women outside the home have increased. Little girls that once played house and looked forward to being wives and mothers can now also anticipate wonderful careers in any field. With mechanization and modern conveniences that are part of our daily lives, it does not require as much time or labor to keep the home. We have appliances that do the work for us with the touch of a button! But it is still our responsibility as women to be homemakers. We are the ones who see to it that our homes are in order and a place of peace and love for our families or just for ourselves! Whether our husbands share in the chores or not, we are to see to it that our homes are kept clean and well maintained.

The top priority in homemaking is the atmosphere in the home. Jesus said, "Peace I leave with you, My peace I give to you;" (Matthew 14:27) Our homes should be homes of peace, not strife and unrest. How do we achieve that with all the turmoil in the world around us and the daily disagreements that are common in any family? We keep ourselves in peace. We find ourselves in that place of peace that Jesus gave to us. He gave us His peace. As we abide in Him, that peace is a fruit of the Spirit that creates an atmosphere around us. His peace diffuses the anger of the moment or the little ordinary squabbles that arise. We must create an atmosphere of peace in the home. In order to keep ourselves in peace we must follow the example of Jesus who went into a deserted place to pray to the Father. We must keep that daily vital relationship with the Father and then we have strength and wisdom to handle any situation. We have our hearts at rest in Him so that we can minister that rest and peace to those around us, especially our families. We live in that secret place found in Psalm 91, "He who dwells in the secret place of the Most High shall abide under the shadow of the Almighty." Our abiding place is under His shadow. That's where we live, so close to the Father that His shadow is over us. That brings peace everywhere we go, especially to our homes.

When we walk in that peace, conscious of the presence of God, we can stay calm in the face of any calamity or hurt or disappointment in our lives or the lives of those around us. We are a source of strength and stability in our homes. We can go about our daily routines with joy and love, rather than hassled and harried like everyone else. Remember, in His presence is fullness of joy! We can walk in joy and love, celebrating each day rather than just hoping we can somehow make it through.

I don't want to sound like a Pollyanna! I know it isn't easy and life isn't all roses and life is hard and cruel at times and we have a real enemy who hates us and tries to hurt us, but I also know in whom I have believed! I know that His strength is mine. His strength is made perfect in my weakness. No matter what the attacks or difficulties I may face, I can do all things through Christ who strengthens me. I want to encourage you that this is how the Father intends for us to live, full of His love and peace and joy! This should reflect most fully in our homes. Our homes should be full of the glory of God as we walk in daily fellowship with Him. We are to be keepers at home, homemakers. We keep the home; we make it a place of joy for ourselves and our families.

Too often the home is sadly neglected as we rush around tending to everything else. We make sure our jobs are covered and we are doing our best there to earn an income. We make sure the kids are on the ball with school and other activities. But we neglect the most important place of all, our homes. Simple things like making a meal or clearing up the kitchen mean so much to life and order in the home. But I have met many women who don't know how to prepare a simple meal or make a bed or do laundry. We have kids from other families at our home all the time who go on and on about the simple meals they share with us. I ask them about their family life and they say whatever they eat is what they put in the microwave for themselves. My daughter is an executive in a large corporation, and she brings in cookies or goodies from time to time. Her co-workers marvel at her baking while they bring a sack of chips to share! Now please don't misunderstand, I'm not saying that we all should be gourmet chefs or perfect housekeepers, but I am saying that we can do the simple things of maintaining our homes. If we've never been taught, we can learn. Especially now with the internet and entire networks devoted to food and home decorating ideas and maintenance help; we can learn how to cook and clean and keep our homes in order. You can just sit and watch TV for a few hours and get ideas on food preparation, simple meals to make, new recipes for old favorites. You can learn how to fix a faucet or vacuum a floor. You can get great ideas on colors and styles for home décor. There is all kinds of help available for us to help us if we have never been trained, or if we just need some new ideas. But when you've watched the television program or found a new idea online, the important thing is that you get up and do something about it! Keep your home!

We've learned about the enemy we face everyday, the devil who roams about like a roaring lion. One of his greatest places of attack is the home. He wants to tear families apart and ruin lives. As women, we can stand on the Word and maintain a line of defense against him in our homes. By doing simple things, like keeping ourselves in the presence of God daily, keeping up with housework and laundry and making meals to nourish our families, we are staving off his invasion. He will have no ground to enter through little areas of neglect that may cause strife. It's one area where we can help to keep the hedge of protection around our families. We can do our part in keeping our homes in order, in peace and in the power of God. This is an important part of being a woman of faith.

❧ CHAPTER 15 ❧
JOSEPH–OUR MIRACLE

With all the difficulties of life and the special demands placed on a pastor's life, we thought we had experienced a lot in walking this life of faith. But the greatest test of our faith came on September 3, 2005 when our son was a victim of a tremendous explosion that completely destroyed the home where he was visiting and killed six children from a family of nine children. Joseph and two of the other family survived. We received a call that night informing us that Joseph was alive and he was on the way to the hospital. We needed to get there right away. We didn't know yet the devastation of the explosion or the fatalities, all we knew was that Joseph was barely alive. We immediately began to speak the Word. As we waited in the emergency room to see our son, we declared "he shall live and not die and declare the works of the Lord." When the doctors gave us little hope for his survival beyond that first night, we continued to declare the Word and the healing power of God. When we were finally able to see him, after several hours of waiting, we could only lay our hand on one place on his body. But we did not allow ourselves to be moved by what we saw: the broken, burned body of our son, we continued to speak the Word of God. His liver had been lacerated, both of his legs broken, his lung deflated. He had burns over 20% of his body. His hair and eyebrows were singed off. His eyes were bloody and he completely lost hearing in one ear. We didn't even recognize our son. But through our tears and heartache we confessed the Word. As we met the grieving mother who had lost six children in that explosion, we put our arms around her and thanked God for eternal life. She declared that God would be glorified in the midst of this tragedy. We would not let the enemy have the victory in this.

Our son Joseph lay in a coma for nearly two weeks. We stayed right there with him, speaking the Word over him every time we were allowed in his room. We put a tape player in his room so that the anointing and the Word could be playing continually, even when we couldn't be there. Every morning as we stood in that room, reading the Word to him, declaring the promises of God, we could feel the power of God and His healing anointing like a powerful Presence hovering around Joseph. When Joseph was attacked with pneumonia, his lungs already weakened in the explosion so that he was on a ventilator to help him breathe, and they really didn't think he would make it, we continued to speak the Word and declare the promises of God. Dear friends and ministers came to stand with us and speak the Word over Joseph, and encourage us with their agreement and faith.

Then after about two weeks, Joseph opened his eyes and began to talk to us. Soon after they got him up out of bed and taught him to maneuver with a walker. His burns were healing wonderfully. And after two more weeks, we took Joseph home! He has graduated from months of physical therapy and is now looking to what God has for his future.

We received a phone call from the manager of the trauma department where Joseph was treated. They had recently been given the number one ranking in trauma units. They wanted to have a press conference and spotlight one patient who they would call a miracle survivor. After interviewing all the doctors and nurses from the different units they all agreed – Joseph Moore was the miracle! There was one nurse who had been in the emergency room the night of the accident and then was on vacation for several weeks. When she returned, she asked about Joseph and came running up to the burn unit to see him. She could not believe that he was alive and getting ready to go home! She said it over and over again – "I can't believe it! You look so good! I can't believe it!" She didn't think he would make it through the night, and here he was sitting up and talking to her! He was a miracle!

I share this testimony to let you know that the power of God is real, the power of His Word is real. When you are faced with calamity, tragedy, or just the ordinary bumps of life – the power of God is real! Faith works! The Word works! This is not just some religious idea that makes you feel good – this is the power of God released in the world to defeat the enemy wherever he may attack. This is the victory that overcometh the world, even our faith! We are overcomers, more than conquerors when we walk by faith in His Word. That is what God has destined us to be. That is what He has made us because of Jesus.

None of us know what the day may bring. But when you are a woman of faith, you know that in any situation you are an overcomer. Life is real, pain is real, loss is real; but the Word of God and the power of faith are more powerful than anything the enemy can throw at you. Lifting up the shield of faith, you are able to quench all the fiery darts of the wicked one.

Rev. Terry Mize says, "I know God is good. I know His Word is Truth." These two indisputable truths can get you through any difficulty. If you know God and you believe His Word, you are more than a conqueror in any situation.

Be a woman of faith!

JOURNAL

JOURNAL

JOURNAL

JOURNAL

JOURNAL

JOURNAL

JOURNAL

JOURNAL

JOURNAL

JOURNAL